What Graeme Goldswo... ...done for "covenant": an ...which traces the profoun... ...~~ ~. ~~~s theme from Genesis to Revelation. This excellent book explains what covenant is, why it matters, and how we cannot understand the Lord Jesus, his work, or his Word without it.

—*David Gibson, Minister, Trinity Church, Aberdeen*

A fascinating little introduction to a complex topic. Jonty's quest to recapture the covenant sweeps us through the whole Bible's story, into the very depths of eternity, alongside profound thinkers across the ages, and right up to present-day Christian living. Engaging, relevant, and often both humorous and thought-provoking, *Covenants Made Simple* sheds new (as well as old) light on some of the greatest mysteries concerning God's wonderful plan of salvation. And while I'd beg to differ on the precise nature of the new covenant, and therefore *who* should be baptized, I'm delighted to commend this book on an often neglected but vital biblical theme. Let the journey commence, if you dare!

—*Dave Gobbett, Lead Minister, Highfields Church, Cardiff*

With all sorts of proposals about what the "big idea" of Scripture is floating about, Jonty Rhodes does us the favor of pointing us to the Bible's own answer to that question. He carefully demonstrates that at the heart of God's revelation of himself to humanity is a well-defined relationship which is given a name in Scripture: covenant relationship. The idea of the covenant shapes the whole of Scripture from the garden to the upper room; and it points us to the significance of the two main characters in the human story: Adam, the first, who was a covenant-breaker, and Adam, the last (Christ), who was the covenant-keeper. Born under the curse brought on us by the disobedience of the former, we are freed from the curse by the obedience of the latter. Jonty's work is clear-headed and heart-warming, satisfyingly biblical and Christ-exalting. I warmly commend it.

—*Liam Goligher, Senior Minister, Tenth Presbyterian Church, Philadelphia*

British evangelical theology has been impoverished over the years by a general failure to appropriate the riches of covenant theology. This is ironic, given that the Westminster Confession of Faith, perhaps the finest confessional statement of covenant theology, was originally a British document. It is thus a pleasure to commend Jonty Rhodes' fine introduction to the subject. I hope that this little book will help many to see the beauty of the biblical covenants and their relevance for God's people today.

    —*Carl R. Trueman, Paul Woolley Professor of Church History, Westminster Theological Seminary, Pennsylvania*

COVENANTS
MADE SIMPLE

COVENANTS
MADE SIMPLE

UNDERSTANDING GOD'S UNFOLDING
PROMISES TO HIS PEOPLE

JONTY RHODES

P&R
PUBLISHING
P.O. BOX 817 • PHILLIPSBURG • NEW JERSEY 08865-0817

ISBN: 978-1-59638-975-5 (pbk)
ISBN: 978-1-59638-976-2 (ePub)
ISBN: 978-1-59638-980-9 (Mobi)

Printed in the United States of America

Library of Congress Control Number: 2014943848

For Georgina and Charlotte

CONTENTS

ACKNOWLEDGMENTS

MY DISCOVERY OF the covenants is almost entirely down to two people: Dr. Garry Williams, now of the John Owen Centre, whose classes both there and previously at Oak Hill Theological College were hugely eye-opening, and Rev. Dr. Mark Pickles, for seven years past my boss and for many more to come, I hope, my friend. I am heavily indebted to both men. Anything useful in the pages to come is likely to have been stolen from them. Needless to say, the mistakes are entirely my own.

I'm grateful to a number of friends for reading through early drafts of the manuscript, especially Matthew Roberts, David Gibson, James Buchanan, and Ted Watts; their comments and critiques have made this a much better book. Likewise, my wife Georgina has patiently read and reread chapter after chapter, improving them each time. Much of the material in chapter 3 I've learned from Dr. Daniel Strange, and chapter 10 I'd particularly like to dedicate to Dan, Jeff, Reuben, and Dave: *tolle lege*, as they say. Thanks too to Kieran Harrod for making my terrible illustrations look professional and editor Eleanor Trotter for her endless encouragements along the way.

Finally, as I hope you'll pick up in the pages ahead, the covenants reveal the significance of the church in God's plan. Most of this material was first worked through with the members of Christ Church Derby, and it's worth you knowing that it is now being published with the permission and blessing of my fellow elders there, Tim Houghton and Matt Newboult.

INTRODUCTION

EVANGELICAL CHRISTIANS are known for their insistence that Christianity is centered on "a relationship with God." Rightly so. But what is the nature of that relationship? I have one relationship with my wife, quite another with my neighbor. My relationship with my daughter could be fairly described as unconditional; that with my boss rather less so.

Covenant is the word God uses to describe his relationship with his people. At each stage of the Bible's story, including our own, God relates to his people through a series of these interlinked covenants. That relationship is more complex than we sometimes imagine. God is a Father who loves his children unconditionally, yet in Corinth he strikes some of those same children dead when they disobey him. Jesus is the Good Shepherd who will never lose a sheep, yet Judas, one of the original twelve, never makes it home. Christ died for the sins of the world, yet not everyone is saved. We are saved by grace alone, yet John tells us we'll still be judged according to what we've done. These examples provoke all sorts of questions in thoughtful Christians. Can I know I'm saved? Does how I live have any effect on how God treats me? Can I lose my salvation? What does God expect from me?

Covenants hold the key to unlocking these kinds of puzzles. I hope we'll see that they bring a beautiful harmony to the different melodies God sings throughout Scripture. Covenant thinking has fallen somewhat out of fashion recently, much to our loss. This book is an attempt to rediscover a hugely important biblical theme.

There have been times when covenant has played a more central role in the church's life, notably during the era of the Puritans—those ministers who came after the first wave of the Reformation and built on its foundations. That's why although our primary focus will be the Bible itself, we will at times dip into the writings of these men and their spiritual successors, to benefit from some of their insight and wisdom.

So, if God's covenants are becoming buried under the sands of time, we ought to start digging. And like any good explorer, we need to first ask, "What are we looking for?" In other words, what is a covenant anyway?

1

THE COVENANT
OF WORKS

Why "Covenant"?

Three years of patient, careful teaching and time was running out. Time and again, he had explained why he had to die, and time and again even his closest friends had failed to understand. Now, only hours before his arrest, the Son of God grasped his final opportunity. Taking a cup of wine in his hands, he thanked his Father and spoke to the Twelve: "This is my blood of the covenant, which is poured out for many for the forgiveness of sins" (Matthew 26:28).

My blood *of the covenant*. Why "covenant"? Wouldn't "This is my blood, which is poured out for many for the forgiveness of sins" have been enough?

Most Christians have at least some understanding that Jesus shed his blood so that we might be forgiven. Far fewer, I suggest, would be able to explain what Jesus meant by calling his blood *covenant* blood. In fact, many of us could put our finger over the word "covenant" and read the verse just the same. And yet, this is the word Jesus uses at the last supper, the final picture given to the men who would become the great preachers of the gospel after his resurrection. The death of Christ stands at the heart of the Christian gospel. And Jesus, for one, thought "covenant" best unlocked the meaning of that death.

Thirty or so years earlier, before Jesus was born, his uncle had sung a hymn of praise to God. As Zechariah looked forward to the birth of his son, John the Baptist, he praised the Lord who was about

> to show the mercy promised to our fathers
>> and to remember his holy covenant,
> the oath that he swore to our father Abraham.
> (Luke 1:72–73)

Zechariah knew that God was about to do something enormous, something that would shake the world. He also knew that the origin of this plan had been the covenant God had made with Abraham right back in Genesis. Covenant is the theme that links the different books of the Bible to make them one united story, blazing through the Old Testament like a firework, before exploding into full color in the coming of Christ.

Even from just these two passages, we see hints that covenant is the concept that will allow the message of salvation God offers to grow naturally out of the story he tells. It is through understanding the covenants that we can move from story to salvation. To press the significance of covenants still further, let's visit the temple, the center of Israel's worship during the days of the Old Testament. If we were to be given a guided tour, we'd begin in an outer court, before moving into a smaller central room known as the Holy Place. Pressing on still further, we'd come to the heart of the temple, the Holy of Holies. So far, so predictable, at least if we'd been on tours of other Ancient Near Eastern temples. They tended to follow the same threefold pattern, leading toward that central most holy place. The surprise with the Israelite temple was what was in this Holy of Holies—or rather, what wasn't. Unlike the nations around them, the Israelites built no statue of their God: in fact he had expressly forbidden it. Instead, we would have found an ornate box, or "ark," containing the Ten Commandments. These commandments constituted the covenant documents of their day. The God of the Bible had chosen to reveal himself not through statues and images, but through covenant.

It's the kind of passages we've looked at so far that move J. I. Packer to go so far as to say that, first, "the gospel of God is not properly understood till it is viewed within a covenantal frame." Second, "the Word of God is not properly understood till it is viewed within a covenantal frame."

Third, "the reality of God is not properly understood till it is viewed within a covenantal frame."[1]

God, gospel, and Scripture: none properly understood until seen in the light of the covenant. Reason enough to begin to dig deeper!

Exactly What Is Covenant?

Clearly, "covenant" is not a word we use much nowadays. Yet, it occurs over 300 times in the Bible, and not just in the dusty corners normally reserved for the intrepid "keen" Christian. The Sunday school favorites of Noah and his ark, father Abraham and his many sons, Moses and the Ten Commandments, and King David of giant-felling fame all not only mention, but are centered on, the unfolding story of the covenant. The great prophets: Isaiah, Jeremiah, and Ezekiel are stuffed full of references to this same covenant, and the psalmists regularly burst into song because of it. But the question still remains: what is a covenant?

Like almost every other Bible word, there's no one place you can look up where Jesus sits his people down and gives them a dictionary definition. "A. Angel: spiritual beings who act as messengers of my Father. B. Baptism: the ceremony where . . ." Well, actually, we'd better leave that one for now. (As we'll see, there's a fair bit of disagreement as to who should be baptized—itself a covenant debate!) The problem with giving definitions is that you could usually give four or five different answers that would all be right. According to Wikipedia, a cow is a large domesticated ungulate of the subfamily Bovinae. According to my friend's three-year-old son Oscar, it's a big black and white thing that moos and makes milk. Both definitions would lead you to a decent understanding of the word "cow."

Similarly, the word "covenant" has been defined in a dozen different ways by Christians down the centuries. This is not the place to get into lengthy disputes as to whose description was the best. For our purposes, I'm going to suggest the following as a simple introductory definition that we'll nuance as we go along: **A covenant is a conditional promise**.

Or, to put a bit more flesh on the bones, particularly in regards to the biblical covenants: **A covenant is an agreement between God and human beings, where God promises blessings if the conditions are kept and threatens curses if the conditions are broken.**

Honestly, you could pick a thousand holes in that definition and add in a thousand other things you'd like to see included.

But by far the best thing to do is to dive in and start looking at the covenants we actually meet in the Bible.

In the Beginning

Perfect. That's how we usually describe the world that God made right back in Genesis 1 and 2. And so it was, in many respects. Leaving aside the endlessly debated question of how long he took to do it, in these opening chapters of the Bible we see God making a beautiful world teeming with life.

Imagine the universe like a play in the theater. On the first three days, God created the scenery that would provide the backdrop to the action. Day one gives us light and darkness, day two separates the sky from the world, and day three sees splotches of land burst out to create continents amid the watery mass that was Earth. Having set the scene, God then turns his attention to the "actors," the characters who will fill each of the three stages he has crafted. So, the sun, moon, and stars are hurled on stage to control the light and darkness created on day one. Day two's scenery of sky and waters is filled with birds and fish on day five. Then on day six come the animals: creepy-crawlies, excitable dogs, herds of wildebeest, all to fill the land that erupted on day three. God is clearly a God who enjoys both forming and then filling empty spaces.

And so to the climax of day six: the creation of humankind. God makes man and woman in his image. We learn elsewhere in the Bible that God is spirit, so it's unlikely that the image of God refers literally to our physical features. Closer to the truth is the idea that we humans are created to reflect some of the character and responsibilities of God. This becomes clear in God's first words to humanity: "And God said to them, 'Be fruitful and multiply and fill the earth and subdue it and have dominion over the fish of the sea and over the birds of the heavens and over every living thing that moves on the earth'" (Genesis 1:28).

God had just formed and filled a whole universe. Now, in their own small way, Adam and Eve were to do likewise. They were to "be fruitful": get making lots more human beings, to form even more images of God. And these children and grandchildren weren't all to stay cramped up in the garden in Eden, but to spill out into the rest of the world, to "fill the earth." Form and fill, just like their Father God.

It's pretty obvious from this first chapter that God didn't just make the world; he also rules it. In fact, it's precisely because he made it that he's in charge. And so, unsurprisingly, as his little images, men and women are to rule too: over the animals, fish, and birds. That's what it means to "have dominion." Under God, they were to be king and queen of the world, caring for and ruling over it.

Which brings me to my first little quibble with describing the scene as perfect. If, by perfect, all we mean is that there was no sin, no disease, no death, no danger, then all's well; after all, God himself pronounces that everything he made was "very good" (Genesis 1:31). But the one thing it wasn't, was finished. There were still people to "create." And did you notice that, as Adam and Eve's family spread out to fill the earth, they would also have to *subdue* it? Subdue is not a word that suggests everything's finished. It sounds very much as if Adam is going to have to do some work. Just in case we were in any doubt, God makes this very point in Genesis 2:15: "The LORD God took the man and put him in the garden of Eden to work it and keep it."

To work and to keep. Adam and Eve were meant to change the world, to improve it we might even say. Not, again, that anything was wrong. It's just that as of yet horses hadn't been trained to pull ploughs. Crops were growing all over the place, rather than more fruitfully in well-managed fields. Trees needed to be chopped down to build houses, boats, carts: it would be tough to explore the whole world on foot! Similarly, it wouldn't do Adam any harm to nip down river into the land of Havilah and craft some of the gold and precious stones found there into a nice necklace for Eve. While he's away, perhaps Eve could carve out some bamboo stalks and begin work on the first-ever flute concerto. So much to do, so many possibilities.

The world that God handed over to Adam and Eve was not a dusty museum that needed to be preserved exactly as it was for millennia to come. No, it was an art gallery full of beautiful white canvases waiting to be made even more beautiful by hundreds of mini-artists created in the Great Artist's image.

These commands are sometimes referred to as the "cultural mandate." They remind us that our work, our families, our marriages, our art, our science are good gifts. They aren't sub-spiritual things to be indulged in during a guilty moment, all the while wondering if we shouldn't really be praying or evangelizing. They are (or should be) ways of making the earth more pleasant to live in, of loving our neighbor with the various gifts and roles God has given us.

Of course, alongside all these positive commands, there was one negative: "And the Lord God commanded the man, saying, 'You may surely eat of every tree of the garden, but of the tree of the knowledge of good and evil you shall not eat, for in the day that you eat of it you shall surely die'" (Genesis 2:16–17). The tree of the knowledge of good and evil was off-limits. And hence, there was a way for Adam and Eve to ruin the wonderful world they'd been given. If they were to steal the fruit from this tree, they would be betraying God, abandoning him as their King and Father, destroying the peace of the garden, and killing themselves in the process. This is the second reason why "perfect" is perhaps not the most useful word to describe the situation in Eden. At this stage, things weren't complete—there was still the possibility of everything going horribly wrong . . .

The Covenant of Works
So far we could summarize the situation in Eden with 3 *p's*: God's people, in paradise, with God present.[2] But the set-up isn't static—something was going to change. And here at last we come to the idea of covenant.

Remember, a covenant is **an agreement between God and human beings, where God promises blessings if the conditions are kept and threatens curses if they are broken.** This is what we see in Eden. The agreement, or conditions, are:

1. Positively, humans must obey God, including fulfilling the "cultural mandate"
2. Negatively, they must not take the fruit of the tree of the knowledge of good and evil

The curse, if the conditions are broken, is spelled out with crystal clarity by God in Genesis 2:17: "You shall surely die." But if covenants also include blessings if they're kept, where do we see these in Genesis 1–2?

Most writers on the covenant have taught that, although it is not made absolutely explicit, there is a blessing promised: that if Adam had obeyed and kept the covenant for a certain period of time, he would have been rewarded. In the Dutch theologian Herman Bavinck's great phrase: "Adam stood at the beginning of his 'career,' not the end."[3] Is this just speculation?

Let me pick two of the arguments used to prove that this covenant with Adam, usually referred to as "the covenant of works," had a reward attached.

The first is an argument from the nature of other covenants in the Bible. Whether it's the covenant with Moses at Mount Sinai, David as he took the throne of Israel, or Jesus and the church in the New Testament, each has a reward as well as a curse. The basic agreement always follows the same pattern: here are the conditions; keep them and I'll bless and reward you; break them and I'll punish you. In Genesis 2, we may only read of the conditions and the curse, but it's of the very nature of a covenant that there be a blessing involved too: curse and blessing are two sides of the covenant coin. In fact there are clues to this blessing in the garden itself. Alongside the tree of the knowledge of good and evil stands the tree of life. When Adam sins, he is banished from Eden "lest he reach out his hand and take also of the tree of life and eat, and live for ever" (Genesis 3:22). Somehow this second tree is connected to the promise of eternal life, a gift taken out of Adam's reach because of the fall, but presumably genuinely on offer had he remained faithful.

Second, as Paul looks back on the story of Adam, he sees a parallel between Adam and Jesus. In fact, so similar are they, at least in the way they relate to the rest of us, that Paul can say that Adam was "a type of the one who was to come" (Romans 5:14) or even call Jesus "the last Adam" (1 Corinthians 15:45). (We'll explore this much more in future chapters, but for now we just need to note that Jesus is called the last Adam because he fulfills the conditions of the covenant that the first Adam broke.)

The significance of this dawns on us when we think of what Jesus won for us. If he earns for us a better reward than simply winding back the clock and returning us to Eden in the same state as Adam, we'll find proof that there was always something greater on offer to humanity.

This is exactly what we do discover. It might seem that things are as good as they can get for Adam. After all, he's just been appointed king, is living in paradise, and has God as his Father. What reward could improve the situation Adam already finds himself in? Isn't Adam already perfect?

But wait a minute—we've already seen that "perfect" is a rather slippery term. Yes, Adam is sinless, without fault. In this regard, he is the same as every other part of creation: and that's exactly the point. Just as the world is spotless but capable of being further glorified, so too is Adam. And just as the world is capable of being corrupted and ruined, so too is Adam. In Eden, Adam is able not to sin. What could be better? It would be better for Adam to be unable to sin! Likewise, in Eden, Adam is able not to die. What could be better? It would be better to be unable to die!

In case that sounds like grammatical hair-splitting, think of yourself standing ready to take a penalty that would win England the next World Cup Final. The crowds are silent; your teammates and banks of photographers look on. Would you rather you were able to score or would you rather you were unable to miss? Surely, the latter every time! Or imagine yourself about to leap out of a plane for your debut parachute jump. Which would you rather hear from your instructor: "It's possible for you not to die here," or "It's impossible for you to die"? Again, a no-brainer. At the beginning of Genesis, Adam was able to score a spiritual goal, but also able to miss; able to live for ever, but also able to die.

Now, let's make the comparison with Jesus. According to 1 Corinthians 15, Jesus makes us alive in a way that Adam failed to do. We know that when Jesus has finished saving us, we will be welcomed back into paradise. The difference is that this time there will be no possibility of things going wrong again. Jesus wins us the reward of eternal, un-spoilable righteousness, holiness, and life. We'll never miss a spiritual penalty, and never face eternal death. We will join him in glorious resurrection life. That is what was on offer to Adam too: if he had remained faithful, then one day the trumpets would have sounded and he would have been confirmed as eternally righteous, the test period over. He would be rewarded with a world and descendants without sin, suffering, tears, or temptation. A glorified world, in fact, that we won't meet again until Revelation 21. And in a glorified world, humanity is transformed to live in glorified bodies (1 Corinthians 15:42–49). As in all the best stories, the end will be better than the beginning.

But we've got ahead of ourselves. It's hard not to, given that Jesus himself said the Scriptures "speak about me" (John 5:39 GNT). But let's recap and summarize this first covenant: "the covenant of works." (Incidentally some people prefer to call it the "covenant of life," or the "covenant of creation." Take your pick—I'm using covenant of works because it seems to be the most common.)

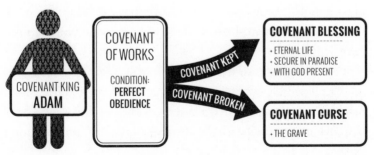

The covenant was between God and Adam, with Adam also representing every other human.

The condition was perfect obedience: positively, to obey the cultural mandate, and negatively, not to eat the fruit of the tree of the knowledge of good and evil. This means Adam could break the covenant either by pinching the fruit or by sitting on his backside and doing nothing to obey God. Both would scar the image of the God role that he'd been given. An Adam who lied to his wife, refused to do any work, murdered his children, and ignored the worship of God, but who didn't eat the forbidden fruit, could hardly have protested that he hadn't broken the covenant.

The curse was clear: death.

And the blessing? Eternal, incorruptible life on a paradise earth, with God as Father and King, and with the potential to sin and die removed for ever.

But wait a minute, the word "covenant" isn't actually in Genesis 1–3. There are several reasons, however, why this isn't a huge problem.

First, have you ever heard anyone argue that Eve wasn't sinning in taking the fruit? I'd imagine not. But the word "sin" doesn't appear in Genesis 2–3. Nor for that matter do we meet any of the Bible's other words for sin, such as "transgression" or "iniquity." But the absence of a particular word is no argument for the absence of the idea, the reality for which the word is a convenient shorthand. So too covenant: word absent, reality present.

That brings me to the second reason: there are occasions later in the Bible where covenants are definitely being established but where the word is not used directly. Most famous is the covenant with David: the account of its formation is found in two places: 2 Samuel 7 and 1 Chronicles 17, with neither passage containing the word "covenant." Yet later writers (such as the author of Psalm 89) are happy to reflect back on them and refer to them as containing a covenant. This is a significant point: we need to let the Bible teach us how to interpret the Bible. We shouldn't be thrown off scent by the absence of a particular word, but instead learn to spot the Bible's own patterns. After all, the other relationship established in Eden, marriage, is later explicitly called a covenant in Malachi 2:14, yet likewise lacks the specific term in Genesis.[4]

Third, Hosea 6:7 seems to call the arrangement between God and Adam a covenant. Speaking about the later rebellion of the Israelites, God says,

> But like Adam they transgressed the covenant;
>   there they dealt faithlessly with me.

Then, there's the parallel with Jesus, explained above. We know for sure that Jesus saves us and relates to us through a covenant: he says as much. It therefore makes sense that Adam's relationship to us is also covenantal. Finally, it's at the very least interesting that, when we do come across the word "covenant" for the first time with the story of Noah, the particular word used suggests that God is continuing rather than beginning to use covenants as his way of relating to humanity. Normally when a covenant is being initiated for the first time it is described as being "cut." But in Genesis 6:18 God "establishes" his covenant with Noah, the "continuity" word strongly suggesting that a covenant is already in place.[5]

All pretty clear, you'd have thought. But some people still seem to get jumpy about calling the arrangement between God and Adam a covenant. John Murray, otherwise a staunch defender of covenant theology, preferred to call it an "administration." Well, OK. I tend to think this is a bit like calling a cow a domesticated ungulate of the subfamily Bovinae. If it's black, white, and moos, it's a cow. If you've got God, human beings, and conditions with an accompanying threat and an implied blessing, you've got a covenant.

So, imagine Adam and Eve as soft-clay figures, slowly hardening. One day, their final form would be set. The question was: would they harden with hands held aloft in worship of God, or become stony figures with fists raised in rebellion? The answer will have consequences not just for them, but for the history of humanity for centuries to come.

2

COVENANT CURSED

HAVE YOU EVER seen one of those "100-most-influential-people-in-human-history" lists? Obviously, they're somewhat subjective—who's made more of an impact: Isaac Newton or Socrates? Buddha or Muhammad? Cleopatra or Margaret Thatcher? Most of the lists are sensible enough to put Jesus at the top. But I've yet to see one that gets second place right. To my mind, there's one individual who should be guaranteed second place on every list, without exception. Barring Jesus, no one has had a greater effect on humanity; no one's life has had more far-reaching consequences. That person, of course, is Adam.

If you're beginning to get the hang of covenant thinking, you should be able to guess what's coming next in our story. God has made a covenant with Adam, with blessings for obedience and curses for disobedience. Adam disobeys. And so, being just, God must punish. God never goes back on his Word, and his Word was clear: "Of the tree of the knowledge of good and evil you shall not eat, for in the day that you eat of it you shall surely die" (Genesis 2:17).

Eat and you'll die. They ate, and so God must come to judge. It's not, therefore, that God has flown off the handle, irrationally losing his temper like a parent who just can't cope with the mayhem any more. God hates sin. He hates it because it messes up his world, like ugly graffiti scrawled across a masterpiece. Because it messes up human beings, the people he loves. But he hates it most of all because it is an attack on him. This is something Satan himself well understood. John Calvin, one of the leaders of the Reformation, wrote the following in his commentary on Genesis 3: "Because he could not drag God from his throne, [Satan] attacked man, in whom His image shone . . . and therefore he endeavored, in the person of man, to obscure the glory of God."[1]

One of the most memorable images of the Second Gulf War was a whole crowd of Iraqi citizens toppling the statue of Saddam Hussein that stood in the central square of Baghdad. Hussein himself was in hiding, but his long-suffering people wanted to attack. In the absence of the man himself, they destroyed his image. Like Saddam, rulers in the ancient world would often build statues of themselves around their empires, in order to remind the citizens just who was in charge. In a sense, this was what God was doing when he made men and women in his image and told them to fill the earth—except of course here the images were of an all-loving Father, not a crackpot dictator. What Calvin helps us see is that, by attacking human beings, Satan was indirectly attacking God. He didn't have the power to kill God; he didn't have the power so much as to scuff up God's shoes. But he could attack God's images, and prevent any more of those images from spreading across the planet. At the very least, he could make sure that any new images would be horribly marred and scarred.

And Adam and Eve went along with the plan. While they were under a subtle attack from Satan, he couldn't actually force them to sin. In Eden, humankind was able to sin, but also able not to sin. They had power to choose either way, and they chose foolishly. Eve took the fruit, and Adam, who was there with her, joined in. They allied with Satan to declare war on God. The action itself might have seemed small—just picking a fruit—but the intent was evil to the core: treason. Despite the gift of a glorious world, all the food they could want, and fellowship with the triune God, Adam and Eve grasped for more. God had been incredibly gracious to them. Gracious not in the sense of forgiving sin, but of stooping down to give them life and entering into a covenant with them that promised even greater blessing. But, like spoilt children, they threw it back in his face.

The dawning that it was a failed plan seems to have come quickly. Our first parents realize they are naked and make loincloths out of fig leaves to cover their sexual organs. (Remember this detail; it's coming back!) Not that sex was involved in the fall. The first sin was taking the fruit, not having sex: sex was indeed the first command, but not the first sin. So, why cover up just these parts of the body? Henri Blocher suggests that it's because they are the parts that remind Adam and Eve they aren't self-sufficient; they are not now "like God" as the serpent had promised. Only God can create from nothing. We need the opposite sex; we cannot create alone. The shame of rebellion and failure drove them to try to hide the most obvious reminders of this fact.[2]

So, covenant broken, the curses fell.

The Covenant Curses

Adam and Eve could very well expect to go straight to an eternity of hell. Except they don't. In Genesis 3, we see not only God's justice, but also his mercy in action. He is gracious, even in punishing. But although Adam and Eve are spared the full weight of the curse, they are not spared entirely.

The curses that do fall are linked to each of the blessings of being in covenant with God which we saw in Genesis 1–2. They are, in effect, the reversal of the covenant blessings, summarized as God's people, in paradise, with God's presence.

People

First, therefore, there are curses related to people. God had commanded marriage and childbearing, so he makes both much harder:

> I will surely multiply your pain in childbearing;
>> in pain you shall bring forth children.
> Your desire shall be for your husband,
>> and he shall rule over you.
> (Genesis 3:16)

Conceiving and giving birth will now be both difficult and dangerous. Marriages will also be corrupted by sin: wives will "desire" their husbands. The same word used for "desire" here is used in Genesis 4:7 to describe sin as a monster "desiring" Cain, Eve's son. Rather than a natural, loving desire, this is a desire to consume, harm, destroy. Similarly, husbands will no longer naturally gently lead and protect their wives, but will instead be tempted to rule as dictators rather than servants.

Paradise

Then there are curses related to the paradise land. God had commanded Adam to work the ground and enjoy its fruits. Now, what would have been a joyful task becomes a far tougher battle between man and nature:

> Cursed is the ground because of you;
> > in pain you shall eat of it all the days of your life;
> thorns and thistles it shall bring forth for you;
> > and you shall eat the plants of the field.
> By the sweat of your face
> > you shall eat bread.
> (Genesis 3:17–19)

Making food and improving the earth will be a case of blood, sweat, and tears, the physical world sharing its king's curse.

Presence

Third, Adam's sin has left him unfit to live in the garden of a holy God: God's presence can tolerate no sin.

> Therefore the LORD God sent him out from the garden of Eden to work the ground from which he was taken. He drove out the man, and at the east of the garden of Eden he placed the cherubim and a flaming sword that turned every way to guard the way to the tree of life.
> (Genesis 3:23–24)

The Second Death

One more curse remains though: the death sentence. In his mercy, God doesn't just execute Adam and Eve on the spot and cast them into hell, as he had every right to do. But he does tell them they will

> return to the ground,
>> for out of it you were taken;
> for you are dust,
>> and to dust you shall return.
> (Genesis 3:19)

These are words spoken at funerals: dust to dust. As Adam had been formed from the ground, so he would return to it. Physical death was inescapable. But there is more to God's words than simply physical death.

When God breathed his spirit into Adam in Genesis 2:7, he became an immortal being. No human being, once created, can ever cease to exist. Physical death, terrible as it is, is just the first death. The Bible tells us elsewhere that: "As for the cowardly, the faithless, the detestable, as for murderers, the sexually immoral, sorcerers, idolaters, and all liars, their portion will be in the lake that burns with fire and sulphur, which is the second death" (Revelation 21:8). Physical death will come, but it is just a doorway: to eternal paradise with God, or to what the Bible sometimes calls "the second death," and at other times, more simply, "hell." Hell is an eternity of being punished by God, and it is here we find the real curse of breaking the covenant of works. When God threatened death, he meant all that that word entails: the first, physical death and the second, eternal death of hell.

We sometimes shake our little fists, as if God is unjust to condemn anyone to an eternity of torment for rebelling against him. The most simple answer to this is: "Who are you to argue with God?" or perhaps even: "What are you going to do about it?" But, more fully, we need to realize the seriousness of our rebellion. The size of the crime is measured in part by the importance of the person you assault. Kill a fly and no one will bat an eyelid. Kill your dog and you might get a fine. Assassinate the Queen and you're in real trouble. So, attack God, the greatest of all beings, the One in whom, to quote Paul, "we live and move and have our being" (Acts 17:28), and the crime is infinitely serious. Adam and Eve are children of God and have turned to strike at their own Father.

So, the covenant curses fell. And yet Genesis 3 doesn't finish on quite such a gloomy note as you might imagine. Adam himself seems to be at least cautiously optimistic. Straight after the final curse is pronounced, Adam named his wife Eve, which means life-giver, because, as verse 20 says, "she was the mother of all living." Why the ray of hope?

The First Gospel
Adam was not a naive optimist, hoping that things would work out in spite of the evidence. Adam *had* evidence: the best possible evidence, God's Word. You see, Adam had been there while God cursed the serpent:

> I will put enmity between you and the woman,
>> and between your offspring and her offspring;
> he shall bruise your head,
>> and you shall bruise his heel.
> (Genesis 3:15)

These words certainly pronounce a punishment on Satan, who had been working through the serpent. But they also do more: they offer hope to humanity.

The first two lines establish the battle lines for the coming millennia. Satan and Eve will fight, and so too will Satan's offspring and Eve's offspring. Satan doesn't have literal children (there's no Mrs. Satan), but he does lead a host of lesser demons. These will continue their master's war on humanity, tempting, accusing, and leading people into sin.

But one of Eve's children will be different. We don't get much detail, but suddenly from the general chaos of the battlefield, we zoom in on two figures locked in single combat: "he shall bruise your head, and you shall bruise his heel." Remember, God is speaking to Satan here. Satan is going to have his head bruised by one of Eve's children. No mention of who that special child will be, only that he will win a decisive victory: to bruise or crush someone's head is to kill them. God is promising that one day a man will come along and defeat Satan. But there will be a cost. In stamping on the serpent's head, the hero will himself suffer. His "heel" will be bruised. Again, at this stage, Adam and Eve could not possibly have worked out the details, but this much was clear: there was hope for humanity, to be found in one future man who would destroy Satan in hand-to-hand combat, while suffering a dreadful, though by no means final, wound himself.

And so Adam had faith. Faith in this promise of God. He expressed this by naming his wife "Eve," whereas up to now she had simply been *isha*, "woman." By renaming his wife, Adam was showing that he trusted God's promise that all was not lost, that salvation was being offered to humanity. He puts that faith into action in 4:1 by sleeping with Eve and having children. He didn't continue his rebellion against God and refuse to carry out his duties. He repented and started obeying again, responding to the command to fill the earth.

And it's interesting that in the very next verse after Adam expresses this faith, God clothes both him and his wife with skins. Previously, they had used fig leaves. Now, God does the clothing, dealing with their guilt. And here we get the first hint that something will have to die: these are animal skins, not fig leaves. Adam has faith in God's promise, repents, and God "saves." This is a pattern that will be repeated many times throughout the course of our covenant story.

Consequences of the Curse

So, it looks like things ended well for Adam as an individual. I strongly expect we'll see him in heaven. But, as we began to see in the previous chapter, Adam was more than just Adam. Adam was a giant. Not literally, of course. Thomas Goodwin, one of the Puritan minsters of the seventeenth century who did much of the deepest thinking on the covenants, once preached a sermon where he compared Adam to a giant towering over the earth, with a huge belt around his waist. And hanging from that belt is every human being who ever lived. Wherever Adam goes, we go. The point of Goodwin's story was that whatever happens to Adam happens to every human being who comes after him. In other words, we are all in relationship with God, whether we're Christian or not.

Goodwin was illustrating the very point made by Paul when writing his own commentary on the Adam story in Romans 5:12–21. Some of the details of his argument are tricky, but what becomes clear is that, as those hanging from Adam's belt, we face three huge problems: guilt, grime, and the grave.

Guilt

First, there is the external problem: we are all guilty because of Adam's sin: "one trespass led to condemnation for all [people]" (Romans 5:18).

I am condemned, or found guilty, because of Adam's trespass or sin. God appointed Adam as what is called "federal" or "covenant" head of humanity. If the head sins, the body sins. There is a connection between Adam and every one of us. It's a link which is not physical but legal, a bit like the president or prime minister of a country declaring war, and all the citizens of that country also being at war. There's no physical connection between him and the citizens, but rather a legal one. So it is too with us and Adam. When he entered into the covenant of works with God, he did so not just as an individual, but as a representative of all humanity. His guilt is therefore legally and covenantally ours.

Our instant reaction may be, "But that's not fair. I didn't choose to be represented by Adam." Well, that's true. But our choice has nothing to do with it. If the president of the USA wants to go to war, he doesn't need each of his 300 million-odd citizens to declare war individually. What he does, his nation does. This is how God has set the world up. We are not just individuals, but joined as a giant family. Non-Westerners tend to grasp this more quickly, being more used to the idea that we are represented by, and therefore responsible for, the actions, good and bad, of our leaders and elders, whether we chose them or not. And of course, the same principle works not just for our condemnation, but for our salvation. In fact, that's the point of Paul's argument in Romans 5. We are guilty because of the actions of one man, Adam. But we can also be declared righteous by the actions of a new covenant King, Jesus. If you want to get rid of the idea that another person can represent you, you're going to undermine the cross, where Jesus hung as your representative. (More of that later.)

Grime

So Adam's guilt is ours. We are born legally guilty. But we are also born grimy. This is the second problem, and this time it is internal, a problem of the heart. It's not just that, on paper, we're guilty because of what Adam did. We are also born with a bent toward sinning ourselves. In fact, we cannot but sin: no one since Adam has been able to avoid sin (except Jesus, of course). To return to the penalty illustration from the previous chapter, those born after the fall are incapable of scoring—at least until we've been rescued by Jesus.

I once had a go at the so-called "sport" of bowls. Now, I enjoy proper sports (defined as those that use a ball: cycling, running, rowing are all means of transport, not sports). Bowls looked to me like the kind of hobby disguised as a sport that was only for those who couldn't do proper sports. How hard could it be to roll one big round black ball close to a small round white ball? Turns out it's incredibly hard. What I hadn't realized was that the big black ball is in fact anything but round. It has a weight in it that means it cannot roll in a straight line, but will always curve away to one side. The pros call this a "bias."

All human beings since Adam, again excepting Jesus, are born with a spiritual "bias." By nature, we curve away from obeying God, curve away from the good path he lays out in his Word. Paul tells us that: "All have turned aside . . . no one does good, not even one" (Romans 3:12). King David can cry out,

> Surely I was sinful at birth,
> sinful from the time my mother conceived me.
> (Psalm 51:5 NIV)

From the first second of our existence, even in the womb, we are by nature sinful.

Together, the facts that we inherit guilt and corrupt, grimy natures from Adam are sometimes referred to as "original sin." Original sin is not a reference to Adam's first sin, but to its effects on the rest of us. The author G. K. Chesterton once wrote that original sin is "the only part of Christian theology that can really be proved."[3] You don't need to teach children to misbehave; you have to train them to do good. Satan has seemingly succeeded in his plan. The sight of God makes him sick, so the last thing he wants is for the true God to be reflected billions of times all around him in holy, loving, servant-hearted human beings mirroring his glory. By tempting Adam to break the covenant of works and therefore pass on his corruption to his descendants, the devil turns the reflections into grotesque distortions, like the magic mirror hall at the carnival.

The Grave

Adam broke the covenant of works, so we inherit external guilt and internal grime. This means we're also subjected to a third trouble: the covenant curses. Because Adam was cast out of the garden, so too are all his descendants. No one today is born in paradise. Because Adam sinned, his descendants are no longer naturally God's people or God's children. And God is not present as Friend and Father to all Adam's offspring. But the curse, as we've seen, goes even further: "Sin came into the world through one man, and death through sin, and so death spread to all [people]" (Romans 5:12).

Death and the grave, including the "second death" of hell, hang over all of us. Our guilt, our grime, and the grave. All will need to be dealt with if we're going to be

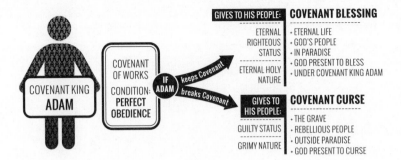

able to live in God's paradise earth as he intended. The serpent-crushing Son of Eve is in for no picnic. When we find him millennia later sweating drops of blood in another garden, before bearing a crown of thorns as he's hanged on another tree, we begin to see something of the horror of the curses of Genesis 3.

But we're jumping ahead in our story.

3

COVENANT CONFLICT

SO, ADAM AND EVE went out into a big, wide, and now hostile world. And yet, they were not without hope, because the very curses God had pronounced also contained the promise that one day the world would be restored to its original paradise. They therefore lived with a tension: faith that God would sort things out in the future, but in the short term, having to face the prospect of life in a cursed world. Alongside this, they now knew they were entering a war zone. Remember God's words to the serpent?

> I will put enmity between you and the woman,
>> and between your offspring and her offspring.
> (Genesis 3:15)

Satan had won round one in tempting the first humans to take the fruit, but God was not going to allow him the final victory. In fact, we've already seen his final defeat prophesied: "he will crush your head" (Genesis 3:15 NIV). Yet God's words make it clear that the climactic confrontation between Jesus and Satan will be just that: the climax of a long-running battle. It's not that everyone will be on Satan's side until Jesus. Left to ourselves, of course, that would have been the case. But God isn't going to keep his saving grace on hold for thousands of years until Jesus finally comes. No, right from the moment Adam and Eve first trust his promise of a Savior, God creates a people of faith, a people who put their trust in his offer of salvation and turn back to him as their Lord. We see hints of this even in Genesis 3:15: there will be enmity, a fight in other words, between Eve and Satan. In the garden, there was no fight: Eve was on Satan's side.[1] But, in his mercy, God changes her heart so she will now battle with her former lord.

This battle will continue in her offspring. Now, "offspring" is one of those words that could refer just to one person or to a group. It's a bit like the word "sheep" in English. If I were to write the (admittedly odd) sentence: "Eve's sheep will battle with Satan's sheep," how do you picture the scene? Some will be imagining a whole flock of horned demonic creatures charging an opposing flock of fluffy white "Christian" sheep. Others will picture a one-on-one combat between just two animals: Satan's sheep versus Eve's sheep. In one of those peculiarities of English, you can't tell from the word itself whether it's one or a group of animals that's in view. It's the same with the Hebrew word translated: "offspring." It can refer either to one or a group of descendants. And in the light of the rest of the Bible's teaching, it seems that this ambiguity, or better still, double meaning, is deliberate.

There is a final conflict and one great Offspring who will do the head-crushing. But along the way, there are others who will continually wage war against Satan and his cohorts. This family of faith that begins with Adam and Eve will continue to trust God's promise of final victory and commit to serve him, rather than Satan, as Lord.

Satan's Kids

So, Eve's offspring are believers: the church, in other words. But who are Satan's offspring? Earlier, I said that they were all the other evil spirits who follow him in his rebellion against God. But there's more to it than that. Jesus shows us that actually many of Eve's physical offspring are in fact Satan's spiritual offspring: "You belong to your father, the devil, and you want to carry out your father's desires. He was a murderer from the beginning, not holding to the truth" (John 8:44 NIV). Jesus is speaking to those who would not accept him as God's Son and their Lord. He teaches them about Satan and then themselves.

First, says Jesus, Satan is the arch assassin. His mission, his driving appetite, is for death. Remember, death in the Bible isn't just about physical death, but eternal separation from God in hell. This is Satan's fate, and he is intent on bringing as many humans as possible with him: he is the ultimate serial killer. But notice how he kills. Rather than marauding around the world with flaming pitchfork as the cartoons would have us believe, Satan kills with his tongue. Jesus tells us not just that Satan murders *and* lies, but that he murders *by* lies: "not holding to the truth." He kills Eve not by stabbing her, but by speaking to her; not with a sword, but with a sermon.

Remember how Satan persuaded Eve to take the fruit. He preached to her. "Take the fruit and you will not die; you will be like God," he hisses. "Sin will bring freedom and blessing. It is God who is the liar and the killer, keeping you from really enjoying life with all his rules. Take, eat. I am your real savior;

I will be a better lord." Satan is a great evangelist, preaching his own twisted gospel. His weapons are words; he cannot force Eve to eat. But like the most depraved killers, he convinces his victims to commit suicide.

Sadly, Satan has many copycats among humankind, and Jesus is bold enough to tell the group of Jews who were rejecting him that they "belong to [their] Father, the devil." John, who was there as Jesus spoke these words, took up this theme when he wrote the letter we call 1 John. He contrasts two offspring: the children of God and the children of Satan. Both were human, but they were distinguished by their behavior:

> By this it is evident who are the children of God, and who are the children of the devil: whoever does not practice righteousness is not of God, nor is the one who does not love his brother. For this is the message that you have heard from the beginning, that we should love one another. We should not be like Cain, who was of the evil one and murdered his brother.
>
> (1 John 3:10–12)

There's a village in Cornwall where, right into the nineteenth century, girls were banned from marrying boys from the neighboring village. Why? Because the neighboring village had a high proportion of ginger-haired men, a sure sign of dodgy Viking ancestry. Even if a young woman's proposed husband was a solid blond himself, he was still off-limits: his lineage was almost certainly ginger-contaminated. To these wise Cornish minds, there was no getting away from the age-old rule: like father, in the end, like son.

So it is with the children of God and Satan. Satan, as Jesus had made clear, was a liar and a murderer. His children, beginning with Cain, are therefore liars and murderers in his image. God, on the other hand, is a God of love and truth. His children can, in turn, be identified by their truthfulness and love, recreated in their Father's image. These two lines, God prophesies in Genesis 3, will be at war. Not, normally, a physical war fought with swords and spears, for the church is not to grow through violence and forced conversion. No, the conflict will be a war of words. One seed, God's, will fight with the message of the gospel. The other, Satan's, will preach any lie that leads people away from God to spiritual death.

In fact, we could even call the battle a battle of "gospels." Gospel just means good or huge news. When a new Roman emperor took the throne, this was announced as "gospel." So the gospel according to Satan comes into conflict with the gospel according to God. One calls us to live for ourselves, reject God, and believe that we'll be happier without him, the same gospel that Satan preached to Eve in the garden and the one we believe every time we disobey God. On the other hand, there is the gospel of God, telling us to turn from Satan to obey Jesus as Lord and have faith in his rescue. This gospel tells us that God, not humankind or Satan, is the source of all truth and happiness. These gospels have been at war since the day God cursed the serpent. One section of humanity will believe Satan's message and therefore grow more and more in his image. The other will believe God's gospel and be remade into Christ's image.

Noah and the Covenant of Common Grace

But it's not quite as straightforward as that, though, is it? I mean, if you're a believer in God's gospel and therefore one of Eve's offspring rather than Satan's, are you *always* characterized by love for others and a complete commitment to believe and tell the truth? And are your non-believing friends really *completely* evil, just looking for any opportunity to bump you off or deceive you with a malicious lie? The answer to both questions is surely: "No." So, what's going on? Is John wrong? Did the battle God predicted never materialize?

In fact, we have to balance the Bible's teaching about two "seeds" at war with its teaching on what has come to be known as "common grace." Now, you won't find the exact phrase "common grace" in the Bible. It's a term that Christians have come up with to summarize the Bible's teaching on this subject. It can perhaps be best explained by looking at the next covenant-related story after Adam and Eve: the account of Noah and his ark.

This story is relatively well known. God sees the horrible effects and extent of sin in people's hearts and decides to come in judgment. The whole earth will be flooded, destroying all life save that of Noah, his offspring, and a selection of animals. There's plenty to learn here of the seriousness of sin, the inescapability of God's judgment, the uniqueness of God's gracious rescue (only through the ark—no one saved them-selves by swimming). But it's the aftermath that we're going to focus on.

> Then God said to Noah and to his sons with him, "Behold, I establish my covenant with you and your offspring after you, and with every living creature that is with you, the birds, the livestock, and every beast of the earth with you, as many as came out of the ark; it is for every beast of the earth. I establish my covenant with you, that never again shall all flesh be cut off by the waters of the flood, and never again shall there be a flood to destroy the earth."
>
> (Genesis 9:8–11)

God makes a covenant not just with Noah, but with every living creature. This is not a covenant like the ones with Adam, Abraham, David, and so on. This covenant has no conditions, nothing for human or animal to do. It's a covenant that doesn't really fit our initial description in fact. It's more of an unconditional promise, never again to destroy humanity or the earth.

This is why it's sometimes known as the covenant of common grace. Common grace is the name given to all the good gifts God gives to *all* of humanity. This is often distinguished from saving grace: grace that provides Christ to die for us and the Holy Spirit to connect us to that death. Saving grace clearly doesn't extend to all humanity. But common grace does. So Judas, Nero, and Hitler all experienced God's common grace. None, we presume, experienced his saving grace. Noah's covenant story teaches us that God is gracious and kind to all, irrespective of whether they repent and believe. God's actions through common grace can be summarized with two more *p*'s.

Provision

First, God promises to Noah that he will continue to provide for the world, even when it fills up with sinners again:

> The LORD said in his heart, "I will never again curse the ground because of man, for the intention of man's heart is evil from his youth. Neither will I ever again strike down every living creature as I have done. While the earth remains, seedtime and harvest, cold and heat, summer and winter, day and night, shall not cease."
> (Genesis 8:21–22)

Whether people believe the gospel of God or the gospel of Satan, God will continue to give them air to breathe, rain for their crops, gravity to keep them pinned. Jesus himself says, "For [God] makes his sun rise on the evil and on the good, and sends rain on the just and on the unjust" (Matthew 5:45). We must remember that even the everyday things in life only come to us because God is gracious. None of us deserves health, wealth, and happiness. Thankfully, God is kind enough to provide them, even to ungrateful humanity who refuse to acknowledge the source. Grace indeed.

Prevention

The second area where we see God's common grace in action is in his restraint of sin. The flood has solved nothing. Just as before the rains fell, every inclination of the thoughts of people's hearts was evil, so after them we read exactly the same: "I will never again curse the ground because of man, for the intention of man's heart is evil from his youth" (Genesis 8:21).

Did you notice the oddity in that verse? God will not curse the ground again *"for"* every inclination of people's hearts is evil. We might expect God to say he will restrain himself "even though" people are evil, but why *because* they are evil? I think the point here is that destroying the world and almost all humanity is not going to solve the problem, because if even one human heart survives, evil will survive too. Wiping the slate clean and starting again gains nothing.

We see this in Noah. Noah is a believer, remember, one of God's offspring, not Satan's. The account of his life deliberately tries to paint him as a second Adam figure, and Noah's rescue almost like a new-creation account. The waters cover the earth again, before receding to reveal patches of land, just as they did at creation. Like Adam, Noah has dominion over the animals and is told to be fruitful and multiply.

But will giving humanity a second chance help?

Not at all. God says that even Noah is not pure or sinless. He carries within him the deadly sin disease. As if to prove the point, a few verses later we find him passing out drunk and naked in his tent, with one of his sons coming in to giggle at him. Hardly God-like behavior.

This story tells us that God's offspring are still sinful. If we just read the John verses about children of God and children of Satan, we might think that it was a case of absolutes: absolute purity against absolute evil. But Noah shows us this isn't the case. For now, even believers continue to struggle with sin. Paul will later write: "For the desires of the flesh are against the Spirit, and the desires of the Spirit are against the flesh, for these are opposed to each other, to keep you from doing the things you want to do" (Galatians 5:17).

The sign that you are a child of God, not Satan, is not that you are free from sin but that you are fighting sin. A tug of war is going on in your heart between the Spirit and the old you, what Paul calls "the flesh." The great news is that the Spirit will win (as we'll see later). But even the fight is an encouragement—a sign of the Spirit at work.

But what about those who don't receive the Spirit? If Noah's flood didn't solve the sin problem, then is every human being who doesn't become a believer going to be as thoroughly committed to sin and Satan as they could be? No. This is the second aspect of common grace: it not only provides, but prevents. It prevents human beings from becoming as bad as they could be.

In his grace, God doesn't let anyone fully give themselves to Satan's project to fill the earth with murderers and liars. Non-Christians clearly do lots of good things, as Jesus acknowledges: "You then, who are evil, know how to give good gifts to your children" (Luke 11:13). See how Jesus holds both original sin and common grace together? We humans are evil, and yet we can do good things. We can give good presents. Non-believing mechanics can fix cars just as well as Christian ones. Atheist doctors can perform operations that save lives. Non-Christian soldiers can sacrifice their lives for their comrades in acts of heroism. All this because God in his grace holds back the full effects of the fall. Common grace: provision and prevention.

Mixed Messages

And so we return to the two offspring. Satan's offspring are not as bad as they could be; God's are not as good as they should be. But fundamentally, there is a conflict. The world will always see two gospels in competition with each other. And we'll do well to remember this.

To demonstrate the importance of keeping both common grace and the war between offspring in balance, think of the last film or TV show you saw. Presuming it wasn't *Veggie Tales* or the *Jesus* film, the writers were probably not Christians. They were seed of Satan, not Christ. Their gospel at root is therefore a gospel of rebellion against God, containing lies that will murder. This will show itself in their film. Perhaps they believe the lie that you can sleep with whoever you want, how you want, whenever you want. The characters have happy relationships, sleeping around, and all seems well. The truth is, the show subtly proclaims, you'll be blessed and happy if you have sex outside God's boundaries.

How do we respond? If we only focus on the offspring-war theme, we'll throw our hands up, declare the film to be satanic, and ban all Christians from watching it. When we understand common grace though, we'll see that there will be some truth, albeit distorted, in the film's message. In this case, it *is* true that sex brings much happiness. The lie is that it's up to us how and when we have sex and that this can give us happiness without God.

If, on the other hand, we completely forget the gospel-war, we may begin to think of films as harmless, providing they're not explicitly violent or sexual. So we assume that PG-rated shows like *Friends* or *Glee*, or even Disney movies like *The Little Mermaid*, are bound to be OK. But wait a minute, there is a war going on, and ultimately there are only two masters: God or Satan. Remember, Satan is interested in two things: lying and murder. He wants to kill you by getting you to stay away from Jesus, the one who gives life. Why you stay away doesn't bother him. If you turn into a murdering, brutal psychopath, great. But if not, he'll happily convince you to be an easygoing, chilled-out "whatever-makes-you-happy" type person, whom no one could dislike.

Satan will sell you any and every lie to make you believe happiness and blessing are found outside of God, and that there are no consequences to rejecting Jesus. Many a little girl has grown up on a diet of Disney to believe that, unless she finds a man to sweep her off into the sunset, she can never be truly happy. Many a Christian girl has gone on to shipwreck her faith by marrying a non-Christian, despite God's commands to the contrary, driven by the fundamental and satanic lie that boys, not God, bring blessing. *Beauty and the Beast* may be low on hardcore violence and sex scenes, but its message is no less powerful.

So, keeping *both* common grace and the continuing conflict clear in our sights will stop us being naive about the world around us. We do live in a war zone. But it is a war zone where God is at work, even among the "enemy."

We've come a long way from Noah, so let's return. After the flood, God puts his bow in the sky as a sign of his continuing preservation of the world. We call it a "rainbow," but the word used is for a bow-and-arrow type bow, an instrument of war. God has hung up his weapons. Ultimately, he will not destroy but recreate the world. The final end of his covenant plan will not be a floaty, spiritual cloudland, but a renewed, beautiful, physical earth. We see this coming about in Revelation 21–22, the last chapters of the Bible. There, the universe is renewed, and humanity and God are reunited on paradise earth.

But how will he do it? How will he destroy sin without destroying all humankind? In fact, God *will* have to kill all those he wants to save and purify from sin. Thankfully, he will not kill them individually, but will do so in covenant union with his Son. Christ will drown under the flood of God's wrath, but rise again from the waters to carry his people into a whole new world.

4

ABRAHAM AND THE
COVENANT OF GRACE

WE'RE NOW READY to explore the second of the three
major covenants that dominate the Bible. The first, remember,
was the covenant of works, given to Adam in the garden. The
"parties" or participants were God and Adam, with Adam
representing the rest of humanity. The condition: perfect
obedience to God's Word. The blessings for keeping the
covenant: confirmation of eternal life in paradise. But the curse
for breaking it: death. Key is Adam's *perfect* obedience—there
was no room for forgiveness or sin.

The covenant of grace, which runs, as we'll see, from
Genesis 3 to Revelation 22, is different. As its name suggests,
this second covenant is not dependent on people's good works,
but on God's offer of forgiveness and grace. The promise to
Adam and Eve of a serpent-crusher has usually been seen as
the moment the "covenant of grace" began, but it is with
Abraham that the terms were first fleshed out.

The Promise

There's nothing particularly special about Abraham. Until God bursts onto the scene in Genesis 12 to make some outrageous promises to him, there is little to make him stand out from his brothers Nahor and Haran. And that's rather the point. (Incidentally, at this stage he's still called Abram, but for simplicity's sake we'll call him Abraham all the way through.) With the covenant of grace it's not that people make themselves into the kind of people God approves of and then he lets them join the covenant. Rather, God, out of his own grace, comes and chooses people who have done nothing to deserve it and enters into covenant with them.

And so we find Abraham minding his own business in the land of Haran when God speaks to him. He gives a command and makes three great promises:

> Now the LORD said to Abram, "Go from your country and your kindred and your father's house to the land that I will show you. And I will make of you a great nation, and I will bless you and make your name great, so that you will be a blessing. I will bless those who bless you, and him who dishonors you I will curse, and in you all the families of the earth shall be blessed."
> (Genesis 12:1–3)

God promises Abraham a people, a place, and God's own presence as blessings. Now, these are not random promises, the first things that happened to pop into God's head as he visited Abraham. Remember, God's original plan was to have a paradise world, filled with people in his image, enjoying life with him. Satan had ruined the plan, but surely that wouldn't be the end of it: God's honor was at stake. Could God be beaten? Was the original plan going to have to be scrapped?

Of course, the answer is a resounding "no." And that's why God makes these specific promises to Abraham, the promises of a paradise land, a people, and his presence to bless them: they are the beginnings of the repair job, putting back in place the very things that Adam lost. It's not the full deal yet. Abraham and his physical descendants are only a fraction of humanity, Canaan a tiny portion of the whole world, and God, while clearly on Abraham's side, is not back dwelling with human beings on earth. But it's a start at least.

The Covenant Ceremony

And so, in faith, Abraham obeys God's Word and sets out for this Promised Land. Skipping over his adventures in between, we'll pick up at Genesis 15 with Abraham now in Canaan. He has been faithful in leaving his home behind, but now finds himself in his supposed "Promised Land" with not a square inch of property to his name and no children; in fact he has nothing but a visitor's permit. God's promises must have looked somewhat fanciful. Even after he'd heard God repeat the promise of a paradise land, Abraham can perhaps be excused for asking, "O Lord GOD, how am I to know that I shall possess it?" (Genesis 15:8). This was a problem not just for Abraham but, if I can put it reverently, for God as well. How could it be guaranteed that things wouldn't go wrong again, that Satan wouldn't throw another spanner in the works, as he had with Adam?

Clearly, entrusting the success of this plan to a man again was a no-go. So, God makes it clear to Abraham that from now on the covenant will be completed not by a man, but by God himself. It will be God who guarantees that the paradise world is restored and Satan's rebellion crushed. Nothing will derail the plan. This he teaches to Abraham in what is at first sight a bizarre ceremony. (It will help if you read the account of it in Genesis 15.)

First, God tells Abraham to take a calf, a goat, and a ram and cut them in half. The two halves are then laid out with a walkway in between. So far, so good. While it might seem strange to us, Abraham would most likely have been unsurprised by God's commands. You see, it was common practice in his day for kings to make covenants with one another. Perhaps, a dominant emperor conquered a lesser king and wanted to set out the conditions for how the relationship would run from now on. The emperor would have some animals sacrificed and cut in two. He would then explain the conditions to the lesser king—each year you will pay me 100 pieces of gold in tax, provide 1,000 soldiers for my army, that sort of thing. If you do so, I will protect your little kingdom and let you remain on the throne. If you don't . . . well, that's where the animals came in. The lesser king would promise to keep the conditions of this covenant and then walk between the pieces of the sacrifices. He was symbolically saying that, if he broke the deal, he would suffer the same fate as the goats—death at the hands of the emperor. It was a grisly reminder of the seriousness of keeping the covenant.

And so, as Abraham laid out the carcasses of the three animals, he no doubt expected that God, the greatest Emperor of all, would call him to promise to obey and walk between the pieces. But in fact, God tore up the script.

Then God puts Abraham into a deep sleep. For what follows, Abraham will be a passive spectator of God at work. The Lord explains that Abraham's descendants will not take possession of Canaan for another 400 years and that in between they will become slaves to a great nation. After that, though, they will return, and the blessings of keeping the covenant will be given to them. But what about the conditions? How was Abraham going to walk through the pieces as he lay paralyzed looking on? Who would promise to fulfill the necessary conditions to make the covenant complete?

> When the sun had gone down and it was dark, behold, a smoking firepot and a flaming torch passed between these pieces. On that day the LORD made a covenant with Abram, saying, "To your offspring I give this land, from the river of Egypt to the great river, the river Euphrates."
> (Genesis 15:17–18)

The smoking firepot is a symbol for God. Astoundingly, God himself "walks" through the torn animals. Get what he's saying here: "I will take on myself the conditions for fulfilling my covenant with you. And if they are broken, I will take the punishment for them. I, God almighty, Lord of hosts, will be torn in two, undergo death, if this covenant is not kept." God signs in his own blood. Remember Abraham's question that prompted the ceremony: "How can I be sure you will give me this great place, all those descendants, and bless me?" God's answer is emphatic: I swear on my own life. What this will entail for God remains to be seen, but already one of the Bible's great doctrines is coming into clear focus. Abraham is saved by grace alone. To say that we are saved by grace alone is simply to say that we're saved by God alone. It is God, not Abraham, who will repair the damage done by Adam.

Covenant Conditions

A couple of chapters later though, in Genesis 17, we come across the covenant again, but this time with a slightly different emphasis. God returns to the deal promised in chapter 12 and inaugurated in chapter 15. Now, it seems Abraham and his descendants won't automatically receive the blessings on offer from God: there are conditions which it is possible for them to break. This should come as no surprise: remember, a covenant is **an agreement between God and humankind, where God promises blessings if the conditions are kept and threatens curses if the conditions are broken.**

> And God said to Abraham, "As for you, you shall keep my covenant, you and your offspring after you throughout their generations. This is my covenant, which you shall keep, between me and you and your offspring after you: Every male among you shall be circumcised. You shall be circumcised in the flesh of your foreskins, and it shall be a sign of the covenant between me and you."
>
> (Genesis 17:9–11)

"You shall keep my covenant." How? By circumcising every male child. In fact, if Abraham and sons don't, they will be cut off as covenant-breakers and not receive the blessings. As God goes on to say, "Any uncircumcised male who is not circumcised in the flesh of his foreskin shall be cut off from his people; he has broken my covenant" (Genesis 17:14). Circumcision has suddenly become a serious business: it is the difference between keeping God's covenant and therefore receiving eternal life in paradise with God or being cast out from all these blessings. But can God really have meant to make an individual's eternity hang on a small surgical procedure? Well, yes and no.

Circumcision is in fact a sign, as Paul explained many years later: "[Abraham] received the sign of circumcision as a seal of the righteousness that he had by faith while he was still uncircumcised" (Romans 4:11). Circumcision is a picture of something else: receiving righteousness by faith. Circumcision is not the big deal; faith is. The real condition of the covenant with Abraham was therefore faith. So we read in Genesis 15:6 (NIV) that Abraham "believed the LORD, and he credited it to him as righteousness."

This brings us to the vital distinction between the covenant of works and the covenant of grace. While both lead to the same blessings (eternal life in paradise with God), and both ultimately have the same curses, the conditions are radically opposed to each other. With the former, people were required to live sinless lives in order to inherit their reward. In the latter, we are not to earn salvation by our good works, but instead trust God to provide it for us. Abraham becomes the model person of faith. He believed God's promises, and was justified, which simply means "declared righteous." While this faith in turn showed itself in fruitfulness—a life of at least attempted obedience to God—this fruitfulness itself was not the ultimate cause of Abraham's salvation, merely the evidence that God's grace was at work. Just like us, Abraham did nothing to merit his salvation. Faith was the empty hand that received God's blessings, not the busy hand that earned them.

Not That Kind of "If" . . .

Now some of you may be thinking I've been trying to pull a fast one here. Having claimed the covenant of grace is, well, gracious, there now seems to be something we have to *do*: believe. Isn't that a kind of "work" in and of itself?

I remember being involved in a university Christian Union mission week. A debate broke out among the members as to whether it was OK to call the week: "Unconditional." "Of course it is," thought the first group. "After all, we don't earn

God's love." "Ah," said the second, "that's only half the story. You only get forgiven *if* you believe." That little word "if" makes all the difference: it brings in a condition. Little though I realized it at the time, this was in fact one of those moments where rediscovering a more covenant-shaped way of thinking would have helped us.

When we compare the stories of Genesis 15 and 17, we meet for the first time with a tension that will run throughout the covenant of grace. In chapter 15, God began the covenant with a ceremony that makes clear that he, God, would ensure that it was kept. One point to the "Unconditional" team. Now, two chapters later, God tells Abraham that *he* must keep it, the condition being faith. One all. So, is the covenant of grace conditional or unconditional? Paul later calls this covenant the gospel, so it's a pressing question. Is the gospel conditional or unconditional?

We're going to have to leave the mechanics of the resolution until later, but already we can see that the answer to the question is: "Both," depending on quite what you mean by conditional. (Stay with me here; we're heading toward some of the deepest waters of the gospel!)

Theologians have distinguished two types of condition: meritorious conditions and necessary conditions. As the respective names suggest, meritorious conditions actually earn a reward, whereas necessary conditions, while still needed, don't strictly earn anything. Meritorious conditions are about *doing*. Necessary conditions are about *describing* things that have to be there for the desired result to come about, but are there through no credit of our own.

Confused yet?

Let's change the scene. Is entry into the stadium for the World Cup Final conditional or unconditional? Well, you only get in *if* you have a ticket, so there's your answer: having a ticket is the condition of entry. But imagine a football fan taking her seat and being quizzed by her neighbor as to how on earth she afforded the enormous ticket price.

"Oh, no problem," comes the reply. "I was given it by my dad for free."

For this lucky sports fan, the ticket was a *necessary* condition: she wouldn't have got in without it. But it was not a meritorious condition: she hadn't in fact earned it.

So it is with faith. Faith is a necessary condition for salvation: no one will enter heaven without it. But it is not a meritorious condition, because faith itself is a gift, earned for us by Jesus and given to us entirely freely out of God's grace. This is why we usually talk about being saved *by* grace, *through* faith. Faith is just about receiving someone else's work.

But what's all this got to do with Abraham? To return to the covenant ceremony of Genesis 15, God is promising that he will supply Abraham with the faith he needs to be counted as a covenant keeper. Faith is not something we summon up from within ourselves, a new work to be performed. No, it's a gift of God. Salvation is really by grace *alone*: we contribute nothing, not even faith. This is the consistent message of the Bible, Old Testament and New.

Even at this early stage of the covenant story, Abraham would surely have agreed with the words Paul would write many centuries later: "For by grace you have been saved through faith. And this is not your own doing; it is the gift of God, not a result of works, so that no one may boast" (Ephesians 2:8–9).

Do you see how this relates to the question of whether the covenant of grace, the gospel, is conditional or not? In terms of meritorious conditions, it's unconditional. If you're talking necessary conditions, it's conditional. Words can indeed be slippery things!

So, Abraham was saved by grace through faith provided by God. And the hints are already there, surrounding Abraham in the form of the bloody animal carcasses, that this is going to be costly faith, purchased by God's own blood.

God's One Plan

Hence the name: covenant of grace. While the covenant of works relied on human efforts, the covenant of grace would be fulfilled by God. As we'll see, the promises to Abraham were really just a foretaste of the plan. Ultimately, this covenant wasn't about establishing one family in a cozy home in the Middle East. No, as we could perhaps have already guessed from the covenants with Adam and Noah, God was going global. He wants the whole world restored, but he'll do it in stages, Abraham being stage one. This is important. The covenant that God gives to Abraham is in essence the same as the one Jesus offers his blood for, the same covenant that saves people today.

We saw in the last chapter that Eve would have offspring who battled against Satan. The offspring theme continues through the covenant with Abraham. In fact, in the New Testament Christians are called the children of Abraham: "Know then that it is those of faith who are the sons of Abraham" (Galatians 3:7). Those who have faith in God's covenant promise, which Paul simply calls "the gospel" in the next verse, are children of Abraham and therefore receive the same blessings he did. But Christians are not given the specific land of Canaan. We are not called to up sticks and move to the Middle East in order to become part of God's people. So, how then can we be "heirs according to promise" (see Galatians 3:29)?

The full details we'll flesh out as we go along, but for now we can see that it is this same covenant with Abraham that God uses to bless all his people, whether Jewish or Gentile (non-Jewish). Whatever our race, if we have faith in the covenant promises, we receive its blessings. But those blessings expand and develop as the Bible story goes on. Abraham was promised a country. Jesus tells us that his followers will inherit the earth. Abraham is promised physical descendants, those who will become the Jewish nation. Jesus says that Abraham's gospel is for all nations. So, in one sense, we inherit more than Abraham was promised. But the "more" is an expansion of his original deal: a paradise, a people, and God's presence.

It's a bit like when you download new editions of the latest software for your smartphone. Is the update the same or different from its predecessor? Well, both really. It's the same fundamental package: a program to make calls, send texts, access the internet, and all the rest. But the later edition is a better version of the earlier one: it's a step forward, while maintaining a fundamental continuity with the original package.

So too the covenant of grace. There are various editions: with Adam, Abraham, Moses, David, and the church. Each

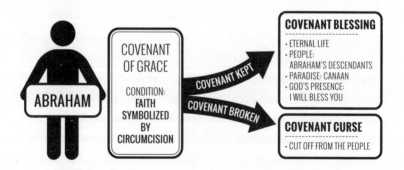

sees a progression and expansion on the last one. But underneath, they are the same deal, the same covenant. They offer the same blessings: a paradise, a people, and God's presence. They have the same parties: God and his people. And thankfully, they rest on the same condition: God-given faith.

5

MOSES AND COVENANT OBEDIENCE

Mapping a Strange Country

The world of the Old Testament can often seem as strange a country as any explored by Dr. Indiana Jones. As newly determined Christians sit down on January 1 to attempt yet again a "Read-the-Bible-in-a-year" scheme, many do so with a quiet dread of what lies immediately ahead. For what can we possibly learn from a time when God's people lived in tribes, fought military campaigns, and followed apparently bizarre food and dress laws? How can these stories say anything to a Christian today, as he sits reading them on his smartphone, sipping a latte, while traveling to work on an electric train?

I want to suggest that covenants hold the answer, and the next edition of the covenant in particular: the covenant made with Moses and the Israelites at Mount Sinai. If we can get our heads around the basics of what takes place on that day, then we'll have a map to guide us through most of the rest of the Old

Testament story, as well as a means to understand how the various twists and turns of that story are still immensely helpful for us today.

Four hundred years have passed since we left Abraham marvelling at God's covenant promises. If we'd had time to travel more slowly, we'd have seen God pass that same covenant on to Abraham's son Isaac, his son Jacob, and then in turn to his twelve sons. It was during the lifetime of these twelve that the family moved to Egypt to escape a famine in Canaan. Egypt, you may remember, was where brother number eleven, Joseph, had become prime minister to Pharaoh, and had thus been able to provide for his family. But, as the book of Exodus begins, Joseph and his brothers have died and a new pharaoh is worrying about the sheer number of their descendants. If he had heard of the covenant promises, he would surely have spotted that God was bringing them to pass: "But the people of Israel were fruitful and increased greatly; they multiplied and grew exceedingly strong, so that the land was filled with them" (Exodus 1:7). Sound familiar? God's plan for humanity, first expressed to Adam in the command to be fruitful, multiply, and fill the earth, was beginning to be fulfilled through the people of Israel.

Pharaoh, though, was unimpressed. Clearly not believing that Abraham's offspring would be a "blessing to the nations," he enslaved the lot of them, setting them to build cities for the Egyptians. Rather like the serpent back in the garden of Eden, Pharaoh tried to derail God's covenant plans. But remember, God had promised to Abraham that nothing would stop him. Certainly no jumped-up king was going to stand in the way of almighty God.

In fact Exodus tells us that "the people of Israel groaned because of their slavery and cried out for help. Their cry for rescue from slavery came up to God. And God heard their groaning, and God remembered his covenant with Abraham, with Isaac, and with Jacob" (Exodus 2:23–24).

Why does God come to the rescue? Why does he listen to the Israelites' cries? Certainly not because they were being particularly godly at the time: rescue is not a reward for good behavior, thank God. No, God comes to save because, you've guessed it, he has promised Abraham that he would. As we saw earlier, he had literally sworn on his life. His own covenant bound him to act.

Covenant at Sinai
And so, we get the famous stories of the plagues and the exodus from Egypt. Fascinating as they are, we're going to move on and join Moses and his people after they've escaped Pharaoh's clutches. Israel gathers around Mount Sinai, where God promises to come and meet with them. Perhaps the most famous section is the giving of the Ten Commandments: "And God spoke all these words, saying, 'I am the LORD your God, who brought you out of the land of Egypt, out of the house of slavery. You shall have no other gods before me'" (Exodus 20:1–3).

Moses reflects on this incident and describes it as the time when "[God] declared to you his covenant, which he commanded you to perform, that is, the Ten Commandments" (Deuteronomy 4:13). The covenant of grace, made with Abraham, gets an update. This time the two parties are God and the people of Israel, with Moses acting as go-between.

Like any covenant, there will of course be blessings and curses attached. Unsurprisingly, the blessings are in the categories we've already met. They're laid out several times, most fully in Leviticus 26 and Deuteronomy 28, but we'll look at the original summary in Exodus 23.

First, God will give them a paradise: "I [will] bring you to the place that I have prepared . . . I will set your border from the Red Sea to the Sea of the Philistines, and from the wilderness to the Euphrates" (Exodus 23:20, 31). Elsewhere God describes this land, Canaan, as a land flowing with milk and honey, where everyone can sit under their own fig tree. Here is a picture of paradise restored.

He will also increase their numbers, in line with his plan to fill the world with people in his image: "None shall miscarry or be barren in your land . . . Little by little I will drive [your enemies] out from before you, until you have increased and possess the land" (Exodus 23:26, 30).

And finally, God will be present with them. Initially, this will be through an angel bearing God's name who will guide them to the Promised Land (Exodus 23:20–21). But this was just a temporary measure. In fact, God wanted to establish a more permanent presence in the middle of his people. The rest of the book of Exodus, chapters 25–40, are almost entirely concerned with this presence. They lay out the design for the tabernacle, a kind of giant tent, God's portable home, to be set up in the middle of the Israelites each time they make camp. Again, there's loads of fascinating detail we could look at, but the heart of the tabernacle project was relatively simple. In a perfectly square central tent, known as the Holy of Holies, God would come and dwell in a special way. Of course, in one sense, God is everywhere, so he can hardly be confined to a tent. But the glory cloud, the fiery pillar, that led them through the desert and in which his angel had traveled, was a special representation of God, showing that he was near to Israel in a way he wasn't to any other nation. At the very end of Exodus, this cloud comes and fills the Holy of Holies as God's presence is shown to be with his people in an even more dramatic way than he was with Abraham (Exodus 40:34–38).

Blessings of paradise, people, and God's presence. But, as you've hopefully realized by now, every covenant involves not just blessings but curses. This is certainly the case with the Mosaic covenant, as the covenant at Sinai is often known. These curses are spelled out in painstaking and terrifying detail in Leviticus 26 and Deuteronomy 28. To get the full story, you'll have to read those chapters, but in essence the curses are pretty straightforward: as with Adam and Eve and the curses of the covenant of works in Genesis 3, they are simply the reversal of the blessings.

> Whereas you were as numerous as the stars of heaven, you shall be left few in number, because you did not obey the voice of the LORD your God. And as the LORD took delight in doing you good and multiplying you, so the LORD will take delight in bringing ruin upon you and destroying you. And you shall be plucked off the land that you are entering to take possession of it.
>
> And the LORD will scatter you among all peoples, from one end of the earth to the other, and there you shall serve other gods of wood and stone, which neither you nor your fathers have known. (Deuteronomy 28:62–64)

First, God threatens to reverse the blessing of being a great people: instead of being as numerous as stars, they will be few in number. God threatens to curse "the fruit of your womb," so they won't be able to multiply and be fruitful. He promises various diseases and military defeats that will actually decrease their numbers. God even prophesies that the Israelites will descend into cannibalism, eating their own children (verses 53–55). These curses can all be grouped under the general category of curses on people, an expansion of the childbearing curse of Genesis 3:16.

Then there are curses related to the place. It will cease to be a paradise land flowing with milk and honey, and instead "the earth under you shall be iron" (verse 23). Crops will fail; cattle will die; rains won't fall. Just as Adam was told that working the ground would be a tiresome, thorny task, the Israelites were warned their paradise could soon become prickly.

Curses on people, curses on the place; there can only be one more threat: the removal of Israel from God's presence to bless. If they continue to break the covenant, the Israelites will lose the land altogether and be thrown out to live in exile among other nations (verses 63–64) just as Adam and Eve were driven from Eden.[1] But, in the same way that the blessings of the Mosaic edition of the covenant of grace were fuller than the Abrahamic, so too are the curses.

This we see in verse 63, where, terrifyingly, God will delight in bringing destruction rather than blessing on the Israelites. In Leviticus, God says he will "walk contrary to you in fury" (Leviticus 26:28). Both passages make clear that the curse which covenant-breakers face is not removal from God's presence exactly—after all, there is no corner of the universe where God is not present. Rather, the curse is that God will be present as an enemy rather than a loving Father.

So the covenant with Moses, edition two of the one overarching covenant of grace, has blessings and curses, as did Abraham's. Back then, Abraham was simply told that the covenant-breaker would be "cut off from his people" (Genesis 17:14). With Moses, the covenant takes a step forward in terms of detail. This is a principle that we'll see all the way through. As time goes on, God gives more and more detail to his people. Although the external form of the covenant and its blessings and curses might change, the underlying reality remains the same. In a sense, we could compare the covenant to a child growing up. From one perspective, a child is the same as the teenager and the adult he or she will become. Equally, there is something new and fuller about the grown person that wasn't fully revealed in the infant years.

What's the Condition?

What constitutes the difference between the Israelites being blessed or being cursed? This makes a significant difference to how we read the rest of the Old Testament. When things go well for the Israelites, what have they got right? Equally, when God does come to curse, on what basis does he do so?

Here, I'm afraid, there is some difference of opinion between writers on the covenant. Broadly speaking, we can put them in two camps. I'll try to explain both, and then you'll be able to decide whether I've plumped for the right one!

1. *Back to the Garden*

Some see the Mosaic covenant as the same in principle as the covenant of works, the covenant God gave to Adam before the fall in the garden.[2] Here, remember, the condition was perfect obedience. If Adam obeyed, he'd be rewarded; if he disobeyed, he'd be punished. There was no room for error, no allowance for forgiveness. Those who see the Mosaic covenant in this light don't think it was ever meant to bring about salvation. They recognize that, as fallen, sinful people, it is impossible to make ourselves right with God again just by obeying commandments. Instead, this group typically empha-sizes that the Mosaic covenant was given purely to point out to the Israelites that "salvation by works" was impossible. Right-thinking Israelites, on this understanding, were to see that they couldn't keep Moses' covenant, and instead look back to the covenant with Abraham for their salvation.[3]

2. Same Girl, Different Dress

For others, and I think it's safe to say the majority of Reformed writers, the Mosaic covenant is the same in essence as the covenant with Abraham. Herman Bavinck, for example, wrote that "the covenant with Israel was essentially no other than that with Abraham . . . The covenant on Mount Sinai is and remains a covenant of grace."[4] This means that the condition was the same as with Abraham, namely faith. Why has this been the majority position in covenant thinking? Inevitably, the debate is complex, but one of the strongest arguments is that the promises are the same: the paradise of Canaan, a huge people, and God's presence. If these were gifts to those with faith from Abraham onwards, it would be odd to make them dependent on works the moment the Israelites get to the edge of the Promised Land. Imagine a father telling his son he would be given a bike on his sixth birthday, and then, come the morning of the big day, announcing that the bike was now dependent on absolutely faultless behavior.

Similarly, there does seem to be the provision for forgiveness of sin even within the Mosaic covenant itself. The book of Leviticus lists all sorts of sacrifices and festivals, many to do with precisely the issue of how a sinful people can remain friends with God. Perhaps, the most famous is the day of atonement described in Leviticus 16. Atonement is to do with reconciling two parties. The English word is a clue in and of itself: at-one-ment, God and human beings brought back together.

At the climax of this sacred day, the high priest would take two goats. The first he killed as a sin offering, dying in place of the Israelites. The second goat is somewhat more fortunate. As the priest lays his hands on it, he confesses the sins of Israel over it and then drives it out of the camp and into the wilderness. Therefore, "the goat shall bear all their iniquities on itself to a remote area" (Leviticus 16:22). Together, the two goats are a great picture of what Christ, the true Lamb of God, will later do for his people. He will take on himself their sins and carry them away, but at the cost of his life.

All of which suggests that there is plenty of grace in the Mosaic edition of the covenant. Like Abraham, Isaac, Jacob, and company before them, the Israelites were called to trust in God's provision of forgiveness and take him as their Lord. In other words, they had to trust and obey; it was a case of repentance and faith, just like with Abraham and just like with us. Faith remains the condition of the covenant. When you look more closely at the Abrahamic and Mosaic covenant, you realize it's the same girl, just in a different dress.

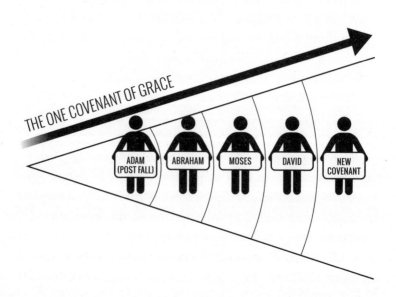

Fruitful Grace

So, what about all the verses that seem to suggest it is through obedience that Israel keeps the covenant? Aren't they proof that the Old Testament is all about keeping the law, and the New all about grace? To quote one that Paul picks up in the New Testament: "You shall therefore keep my statutes and my rules; if a person does them, he shall live by them: I am the LORD" (Leviticus 18:5). If you do this, you'll live. Seems pretty straightforward, doesn't it? Surely a knock-down text for those advocating a "back-to-the-garden" view mentioned above? In fact, I'd suggest not. Consider some other verses:

> For by your words you will be justified, and by your words you will be condemned.
> (Matthew 12:37)

> Was not Abraham our father justified by works when he offered up his son Isaac on the altar?
> (James 2:21)

> [God] will render to each one according to his works: to those who by patience in well-doing seek for glory and honor and immortality, he will give eternal life.
> (Romans 2:6–7)

Now, notice that all these verses come from the New Testament: the first from Jesus, the second from his half-brother James, the third from Paul. No one thinks that Jesus, James, or Paul preached a gospel of salvation by works. All are perfectly clear that it is only through faith and by grace that we can be saved. So, why are they suddenly talking as if our works or our words "justify" us? (Remember, to be justified is to be declared righteous by God.)

The answer is that true faith is always accompanied by obedience. Not perfect obedience, certainly, but obedience nonetheless. Faith is a gift of God after all, a gift of God's grace. And when God gives this saving, faith-giving grace to his people, he also gives life-changing grace. He gives us the gift of the Holy Spirit who makes us "born again." This new life is a life of obedience to God, not as a means of obtaining salvation—that's already been given—but as a sign that we have received the gift.

Think of two fruit trees. One is dead, one alive. How can you tell? By the fruit, of course. The living tree will bear fruit; the dead one will not. Now, does the fruit *make* the first tree alive? No. Stapling apples onto a dead tree achieves nothing. But fruit is the evidence that the tree possesses the gift of life. If a gardener was coaching his young apprentice how to root out and destroy all the dead trees in an orchard, he might well point to a healthy apple tree and say something like, "This is a live one, because it's got fruit on it." If he was being strictly accurate, the tree isn't alive *because* of its fruit, but because of its roots, leaves, and functioning photosynthetic processes. But a live tree is identified by good fruit.

And so, Jesus can say, "By your words you will be justified," and James can tell us we are justified by works. They don't mean that our actions *make* us justified. They mean that they are the proof we are justified, evidence proving the underlying reality. It is exactly the same with the Mosaic covenant. When God says in Leviticus, "Do this and live," he doesn't mean that strict obedience to the commandments will *make* people alive eternally. No, obedience is the evidence that they are alive, exactly the same principle as Paul's argument: "God will give you eternal life if you do well" (see Romans 2:6).

The story of the exodus gives us a great picture of all this. God didn't sneak in among the chain gangs as the Israelites honored away, slip them a copy of the Ten Commandments, and then promise he'd return to rescue them if they kept the rules. No, rescue came first, and the rules followed as a way of living out their new life of freedom in God's service.

It is exactly the same pattern as the Abrahamic covenant. Sometimes people try to play Abraham and Moses off against each other as if Abraham was all about grace and Moses all about works. But God told Abraham to "walk before me, and be blameless" (Genesis 17:1). He commanded him to leave his homeland and family, and travel. Abraham's covenant was just as much one of obedience as that of Moses. As has often been said, we are saved by faith alone, but saving faith is never alone. Trees watered by the streams of God's grace always bear fruit.

The Purpose of Obedience

Why all the focus on obedience then? Remember, God's aim is not simply a world full of any old people: he wants a world full of people in his image. The law, summarized by the Ten Commandments, lets us know what that will look like.

We can now see why obedience was and is so important. There are three main reasons. First, and most importantly, it honors the God who has rescued us. Second, if we had time to stop off in the Psalms, we might see that it also brings great joy to us. David can write that "the precepts of the LORD are right, rejoicing the heart" (Psalm 19:8), and the apostle John tells us that God's commands are not a burden (1 John 5:3). God's rules aren't there to make life difficult for us; they are to help us enjoy life as it was meant to be. Obedience brings blessing, as we've already seen.

But there's one more reason for obedience. As well as honoring God and blessing us, it also blesses the world around us.

> Now therefore, if you will indeed obey my voice and keep my covenant, you shall be my treasured possession among all peoples, for all the earth is mine; and you shall be to me a kingdom of priests and a holy nation. These are the words that you shall speak to the people of Israel.
> (Exodus 19:5–6)

Obedient Israel would be a "kingdom of priests" and a "holy nation." Priests are go-betweens between God and people. The idea was that, as Israel trusted God and showed this trust by obeying the Ten Commandments and other laws, they would stand out from the pagan nations around them. The other nations would see Israel as different, and be attracted toward them—and therefore to God. So, Israel's worship was also a witness. Again, this is not a new theme: Abraham was told that his descendants would be a blessing to the nations.

Peter picks up on this aspect of the covenant with Moses and applies it to Christians: "But you are a chosen race, a royal priesthood, a holy nation, a people for his own possession, that you may proclaim the excellencies of him who called you out of darkness into his marvellous light" (1 Peter 2:9).

Christians don't have priests; we *are* priests, all of us. We are to stand out from the world through our behavior, as those who have been set free not from Egypt, but from the "darkness" of not knowing God. Why?

"Keep your conduct among the Gentiles honorable, so that when they speak against you as evildoers, they may see your good deeds and glorify God on the day of visitation" (1 Peter 2:12).

Holiness is mission-minded. We are meant to stick out like a sore thumb.

I remember arriving in JFK Airport in New York with a friend who had never seen an Orthodox Jew before. He was so startled by them, with their curled hair, robes, long beards, and headgear, that he actually stopped and pointed! Those who keep to the strict dress codes of the Mosaic covenant do stand out. We'll return to the question of why we no longer keep these kinds of rules later. But for now, we should remember that our behavior as Christians should make us seem just as different (and perhaps just as odd) to non-believers around us as the various clothing and dress laws of Judaism do. People should stop and point.

The covenant forms a community of people who are different from the world around, and right from day one that means opposition. Back in Genesis 12, Abraham was told by God that "him who dishonors you I will curse" (v. 3). Not everyone is going to be in the Abraham fan club. Sometimes, there is pressure for the church to try to become more relevant, more suitable for the twenty-first century. Invariably, this means giving up some of God's holiness laws, most often loosening the call for sexual purity. "We need to show people that we're normal, like them," the line goes. In fact this is completely wrong-headed. When God saves people, he saves them to be different. It is that difference, that strangeness, that attracts people, albeit while driving some others away at the same time. Yes, Peter acknowledges, some will speak against you. Jesus said the same thing: "Blessed are you when people hate you and when they exclude you and revile you and spurn your name as evil, on account of the Son of Man!" (Luke 6:22). If the church is following Jesus, then it will be known, at least in some quarters, as evil! When this happens, as is increasingly

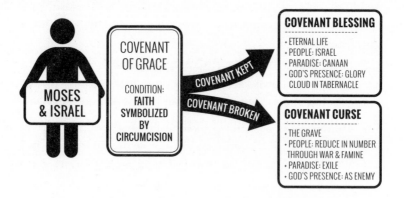

the case in the West, then don't panic, says Jesus. And certainly don't change to fit in: spiritual chameleons are no use to anyone. No, stay faithful to your Lord, and keep going. Covenant faithfulness will eventually end in blessing.

So, how will Israel do in the light of such awesome covenant privileges? We'll soon find out.

6

DAVID AND THE COVENANT KING

From Sinai to Saul

Since we left Moses and the Israelites at Sinai, a lot has happened. Moses has died, just before he could enter Canaan, and handed over leadership to Joshua. Joshua, as the book that bears his name relates, leads the Israelites in a largely successful conquest of the Promised Land. The next book of the Bible, Judges, tells us of the earliest days of living in the land. As the Israelites try to complete their conquest, they go through phases of being faithful to God, but then long periods of ignoring him. If you imagine their obedience being measured on a line graph, while there would be the odd positive upward turn, on the whole the trend would be downwards. Why did Israel find it so hard to obey?

We don't know who wrote Judges, but whoever it was had a message for later readers, a message the writer makes clear in the last verse of the book: "In those days there was no king in Israel. Everyone did what was right in his own eyes" (Judges 21:25).

82 | COVENANTS MADE SIMPLE

On the whole, the period of the Judges (the name given to the different leaders of Israel at this time) was a period of covenant breaking. Far from listening to God, "Everyone did what was right in his own eyes." As you'd expect, this disobedience resulted in God punishing them. Time and again, enemies would attack and defeat Israel, and subject them to slavery.

The author of Judges has an explanation for this though: "In those days there was no king in Israel." If only there had been a godly king, perhaps things would have gone better.

In one sense, the Israelites shouldn't have needed a king to keep them in line. God's Word should have been enough. And the last thing they needed was "a king to judge [them] like all the nations," as they later demand (1 Samuel 8:5). If they were to have a king, surely he was meant to be *different* from the kings of other nations? But it seems that a king was, in principle, a good idea. Judges certainly leads us to think that way, and God had in fact already put in place rules for the kind of king Israel was to have. In Deuteronomy 17, he instructs the Israelites to make sure they pick a fellow Israelite brother to rule over them, rather than a foreigner. The king himself must avoid the three Gs: guns, gold, and girls (OK, not guns exactly, but horses were for pulling chariots, the leading weapon of 1200 BC).[1]

The reason for this is that, if the king did start amassing all these things, he would become a king like the other nations. Central to this is that he must not "cause the people to return to Egypt" (Deuteronomy 17:16). God had gone to a lot of trouble to get the people out of Egypt and make them into a kingdom of priests, a light to the Gentiles. The last thing he needed was a king trying to lead a spiritual reversal of all the exodus had achieved.

No, the king must lead the way in holiness. In order to ensure this, each king was to write out his own copy of the law of God, have it checked by the Levites to make sure it was accurate, and then meditate on it day and night throughout his reign. God's Word would be the real power behind the throne.

This was one of the things that went wrong with Saul, Israel's first choice of king. Saul was just the kind of king Egypt might have chosen: handsome, tall, and a great warrior. But he was not one to take too much notice of God's Word. Throughout 1 Samuel, Saul continually fails to listen to God as he speaks through the prophet Samuel. And so, eventually, Saul is replaced by David.

The Missing Piece

David had no royal pedigree. When we first meet him he is a shepherd boy, spending long days and nights living rough out in the fields, guarding his family's sheep. But God chooses him to be king and, through the prophet Nathan, establishes a covenant with him:

> And I have been with you wherever you went and have cut off all your enemies from before you. And I will make for you a great name, like the name of the great ones of the earth. And I will appoint a place for my people Israel and will plant them, so that they may dwell in their own place and be disturbed no more. And violent men shall afflict them no more, as formerly.
> (2 Samuel 7:9–10)

The language may remind you of God's promises to Abraham. If so, you're quite right: God is further developing his one covenant plan. So, we see a promise that God's people will live in safety in God's paradise, free from their enemies. A few verses later, God promises his presence to dwell among them permanently, no longer just in the temporary tent of the tabernacle, but in a far grander temple. People, paradise, and presence. So what's new?

What's new is David. From now on, the people's destiny will be interwoven with the destiny of one family. David is the first of this family, but his place will be taken by his son, and his son after that:

> When your days are fulfilled and you lie down with your fathers,
> I will raise up your offspring after you, who shall come from your
> body, and I will establish his kingdom. He shall build a house for
> my name, and I will establish the throne of his kingdom for ever.
> I will be to him a father, and he shall be to me a son.
> (2 Samuel 7:12–14)

David's offspring will be the rulers of Israel from now on. Each of the promises of paradise, people, and God's presence are repeated to him. He will have a kingdom to rule—that's the people and the paradise. And God will be with him. In fact, so close will the relationship be that David and his descendants will be called sons of God. God will be present with them as Father.

So, now we have a fourth element to add to the covenant of grace: God appoints a covenant king. In a way, this isn't a completely unexpected development: back in Eden, Adam was told to rule over all creation. He was meant to be king over humanity, but blew it. Abraham had been promised that some of his descendants would be kings (Genesis 17:6), but so far we've not seen any sign of them. Here, God continues to undo the damage of the fall, by appointing David and his descendants as covenant kings. The missing piece of the covenant jigsaw is in place.

Which King?

2 Samuel 7 establishes God's covenant with David. It is, in essence, the same covenant as with Abraham and Moses, the covenant of grace, but now with the added dimension of kingship. Like the earlier editions, therefore, it also has "conditions":

> The LORD swore to David a sure oath
>   from which he will not turn back:
> "One of the sons of your body
>   I will set on your throne.
> If your sons keep my covenant
>   and my testimonies that I shall teach them,
> their sons also for ever
>   shall sit on your throne."
> (Psalm 132:11–12)

If your sons *keep* the covenant. There's the condition. Solomon, David's son, and all further descendants must stay faithful to God's covenant and testimonies. If they do, they'll keep the throne. If not, they'll be punished.

How exactly the kings are to keep the covenant is not explicitly stated here, but the deal is essentially the same as with all the former covenant editions. David and company are to trust God's promise and take him as their Lord, living as he commands them. The "testimonies" of the Lord in verse 12 most likely refer back to the law given under Moses—primarily the Ten Commandments and those specific king-related rules back in Deuteronomy 17. So, the king had to keep his covenant in the same way as Israel had to before, by taking God as their Savior and Lord.

But is the covenant really conditional? In verse 11, God swears "a sure oath from which he will not turn back" that at least one of David's children will rule. That sounds pretty certain to me. OK, along the way, the odd son-king might go astray, but there is simply no doubt that one day a faithful king will rule for ever. It's as certain as God's promise to Abraham that he would have as many children as there are stars in the sky, and that those children would inherit the paradise of Canaan. So, we seem to have come to the same tension as we did with the covenant with Abraham. On the one hand, it has conditions; on the other, God promises that the blessings will come, that "curse" will not win. We're nearly there, but for now we're not going to resolve the tension. First, we'll see how the covenant plan plays out from David onwards.

The First Son
David's son Solomon takes to the throne, and initially all is well.

> Judah and Israel were as many as the sand by the sea. They ate and drank and were happy. Solomon ruled over all the kingdoms from the Euphrates to the land of the Philistines and to the border of Egypt. They brought tribute and served Solomon all the days of his life.
> (1 Kings 4:20–21)

See the promises being fulfilled? The people of Israel are as many as the sand by the sea, just as God promised Abraham in Genesis 22. They are living in the land stretching from the Euphrates to Egypt, just as God promised Abraham in Genesis 15. Solomon is ruling over them, as a wise father. People, paradise, the covenant king, but what about God's presence?

In fact, this blessing too is lavished on Israel during Solomon's reign. The early chapters of 1 Kings tell of the building of a great temple for God. Solomon oversees the building and recognizes its significance. On the day of its dedication, "a cloud filled the house of the LORD, so that the priests could not stand to minister because of the cloud, for the glory of the LORD filled the house of the LORD" (1 Kings 8:10–11). God comes in his glory cloud to fill the temple with his presence, just as he had done the tabernacle before. Solomon knows what's going on:

> O LORD, God of Israel, there is no God like you, in heaven above or on earth beneath, keeping covenant and showing steadfast love to your servants who walk before you with all their heart, who have kept with your servant David my father what you declared to him. You spoke with your mouth, and with your hand have fulfilled it this day.
>
> (1 Kings 8:23–24)

God is keeping his covenant. He has established his people in the land, given them a wise king, and now he is present in their midst. It's a high point of Israel's history. Soon, the Queen of Sheba arrives to marvel at Solomon's wealth and wisdom. She comes bearing gifts, but leaves even more heavily laden. Even the nations are now being blessed, and all in line with God's promise to Abraham. We learn that "the whole earth sought the presence of Solomon to hear his wisdom, which God had put into his mind" (1 Kings 10:24). Truly, God keeps his promises.

The Fading Light

But sadly, it's not going to last. God's kingdom is not going to find its fulfillment in Solomon. Soon, in fact, Solomon is committing exactly the sins which Deuteronomy 17 warned against. He imports horses and chariots from Egypt, marries an Egyptian princess, adds another 700 wives and 300 concubines, and stockpiles gold beyond belief. Guns, girls, and gold: they're all there. And lo and behold, "when Solomon was old his wives turned his heart after other gods, and his heart was not wholly true to the LORD his God" (1 Kings 11:4).

Solomon has not kept the testimonies of the Lord as the covenant dictated. The covenant sanctions will therefore fall. God appears to Solomon a final time:

> Therefore the LORD said to Solomon, "Since this has been your practice and you have not kept my covenant and my statutes that I have commanded you, I will surely tear the kingdom from you and will give it to your servant. Yet for the sake of David your father I will not do it in your days, but I will tear it out of the hand of your son. However, I will not tear away all the kingdom, but I will give one tribe to your son, for the sake of David my servant and for the sake of Jerusalem, which I have chosen."
> (1 Kings 11:11–13)

We need to be careful here. It's not that God brings the fullness of the covenant curses to bear on Solomon. In fact, both the Mosaic and Davidic covenants have a sliding scale of punishments. Compare Israel's covenant role as a light to the Gentiles less to a simple on/off light and instead to one of those dimmer switches. At base, yes, the light is on or off: you have faith or you don't. But obedience after that can grow or dim. When the Israelites' light began to fade, God in his love would send a warning sign, a small foretaste of the fuller curses—warning bells to wake his people up before the light is completely extinguished.

Speaking about David's descendants, God had cautioned: "When he commits iniquity, I will discipline him with the rod of men, with the stripes of the sons of men, but my steadfast love will not depart from him" (2 Samuel 7:14–15). This disciplining aspect of life under the covenant is one to which we will return. At this stage of the story though, notice that the consequences aren't just for Solomon. Because of this one man's disobedience, the nation will be torn in two. Just as we saw earlier, the people's fate now lies in the hands of their king. While Solomon kept the covenant, the people were blessed. When Solomon rebels, disaster falls on his whole people.

Yet the covenant plan must continue. God cannot totally destroy the Israelites, or completely eradicate the line of covenant kings. After all, he had sworn to David that his offspring would certainly rule. Throughout the rest of the book of Kings, we see a succession of rulers come and go. Some are faithful; most are rebellious.

Kingdom Collapse

After Solomon, the kingdom does indeed get torn in two. His son Rehoboam keeps Jerusalem and the two southern tribes of Benjamin and Judah. He therefore keeps the palace and temple, so the Levites all move south to join him. But the ten northern tribes rebel and form a breakaway state. Confusingly, this northern kingdom is known as "Israel," with its capital Samaria. The southern kingdom is known as Judah.

The kings of this new Israel are not descended from David and are soon in full-scale rebellion from God. Not being inheritors of the covenant promise, they have no hope of seeing their line established on the throne. King and people consistently break the covenant. God continues to warn them, through prophets and through implementing the covenant curses laid out at Sinai. In 2 Kings 6, we even read of Israelites eating their own children, surely a sign that the end is near. Eventually, the entire nation is defeated by the Assyrians, who take thousands of the Israelites into exile and in their place bring people from Babylon and other enemy nations to dwell in the land. It is these immigrants who intermarry with the remaining Israelites who become the Samaritans of Jesus' day, named after Samaria, their capital.

Things go somewhat better in Judah, the southern kingdom where the Davidic line continues unbroken. Every now and then, a faithful king pops up and restores some degree of order to the worship of the Lord. Even this doesn't last though. A king named Manasseh comes to the throne and is so steeped in idolatry that God's patience runs out:

> And the LORD said by his servants the prophets, "Because Manasseh king of Judah has committed these abominations and has done things more evil than all that the Amorites did, who were before him, and has made Judah also to sin with his idols, therefore thus says the LORD, the God of Israel: Behold, I am bringing upon Jerusalem and Judah such disaster that the ears of everyone who hears of it will tingle."
>
> (2 Kings 21:10–12)

Manasseh brings covenant curses down on his people in two ways. First, he does so as their representative. It is because *he* sins that God will judge. As their covenant king, his record gives God grounds to punish his whole people. In a sense, they bear the guilt of his crimes. But equally, Manasseh "made Judah also to sin with his idols." Here, the problem is not Manasseh's lack of righteousness, but his corrupting effect on his people. Through his influence, they too indulge in grimy, sinful lives.

This might sound familiar. It is an echo of Adam in the garden. When Adam sinned, remember, he did so as covenant king of all humankind. Through being united to him, we become corrupt too. Adam and Manasseh both teach us that, in order to be saved, we'll need a covenant king who can give us a righteous rather than a guilty status, one who can give us pure rather than grimy hearts.

Josiah, Manasseh's grandson, leads a brief revival, but, during the reigns of his various sons, the covenant curses fall with a vengeance. The last two chapters of 2 Kings lay out the near-total unpicking of the covenant blessings. The paradise land is struck with a famine so severe that no one can eat. Thousands of people are carried off into exile in Babylon. The covenant king himself is dethroned and imprisoned. And perhaps most horrific of all, God's temple, the place of his presence, is destroyed. People, paradise, God's presence, and the covenant king all lie in tatters; what now for the great plan of restoration? Are we not back in Genesis 3? What progress have we really made?

A Glimmer of Light
Well, one thing has progressed. People don't seem to have got much better, and the world is more or less in the same state, but there is one huge, game-changing difference: God has made covenant promises. A glimmer of hope remains. The Old Testament has shown us generation after generation of covenant-breakers, both kings and commoners. We know that covenants have conditions, and curses if broken. But we've seen too that God seems strangely confident that the covenant

plan *will* end in blessing, not curse. He swore to Abraham that his people would be established in the land and swore to David that one of his offspring would rule. How can this be when more or less everyone is unfaithful to the covenant? We've yet to discover. But that he will rule is in no doubt.

This becomes the hope of faithful Jews in exile. They know God's promises to David. Even though they themselves might not be in line to be the next Davidic king, a king means a kingdom, and a kingdom means people and a place. God must restore Israel to the land or he will have broken his promise to David, not to mention Abraham. And so, the Jews sing psalms like Psalm 89:

> [The LORD says]
> I will not remove from him my steadfast love
>   or be false to my faithfulness.
> I will not violate my covenant
>   or alter the word that went forth from my lips.
> Once for all I have sworn by my holiness;
>   I will not lie to David.
> His offspring shall endure for ever,
>   his throne as long as the sun before me.
> Like the moon it shall be established for ever,
>   a faithful witness in the skies.
> But now you have cast off and rejected;
>   you are full of wrath against your anointed.
> (Psalm 89:33–38)

The last lines show us that, at the time of writing, all was not well. Perhaps the writer was in exile. Perhaps, under siege in Jerusalem. Either way, it was a period of covenant-breaking and covenant curses, rather than covenant obedience and covenant blessings. Yet, the psalmist remains optimistic. He is trusting in God's "steadfast love." This isn't just a vague notion that God is kind of loving, so he will probably sort things out in the end. The reason why the psalmist is confident of God's steadfast love is because God promised it to David when he made a covenant with him. The phrase "steadfast love" translates a Hebrew word, *Ḥesed*, which is almost always used in the context of the covenant. God has sworn that he will show his love to David by establishing David's kingdom, albeit with one of his descendants. The Jews could therefore be certain that one day they'd be rescued and could plead the covenant promises back to God. They pray, in effect, "May your king come," knowing that the king will be given a kingdom. Their great hope is not to be the king, but to be part of that kingdom. Everything therefore rests on the king.

This phase of covenant history has plenty to teach us. In a sense, we too remain in exile, strangers in the world outside of Eden, whose hope is the return of the King. But what gives us certainty that that great day will arrive? God's covenant promise that Jesus will inherit the earth and a people beyond number. So, with the psalmist, we can take those promises and pray them back to God, fully confident that he will be faithful to his Son and to his Word.

7

THE NEW COVENANT

TODDLERS MAKE A MESS. Lucas, being three, is no exception. While he may grow up to be Derby's answer to Rembrandt, for now, give him a paintbrush and pot and the result will be more "modern art" than masterpiece. Or it was, that is, until mother Zoe came up with a solution. Instead of giving Lucas real paint, she now gives him a bucket filled with water and sends him outside to paint away to his heart's content. As he happily slaps water all over the place, things change color—or at least seem to. But, of course, nothing's really changing; it's just a temporary covering until the water dries up, after which everything is exactly as it was before.

So far in our covenant story, we might almost be tempted to accuse God of being as effective as three-year-old Lucas. Sure, he throws some promises around, makes the odd dramatic intervention, but does anything really change?

As we left Israel at the end of the Old Testament, God's people were scattered, his presence had left the temple, and the land was in ruins. Something had to change. And what does God do? He comes and makes another covenant promise: "I will remember my covenant with you in the days of your youth, and I will establish for you an everlasting covenant" (Ezekiel 16:60). It was time for a new edition, but this time things would be different. This was an "everlasting covenant": it would be the final installment, stretching off into eternity. Other prophets refer to it as the "new covenant." We'll return to just what's new about it later, but Ezekiel shows us it's not totally new. God makes it on the back of the covenant at Sinai, the "covenant with you in the days of your youth," as he calls it here. So, this new covenant would have its roots in the covenants that have gone before: it would be part of the covenant of grace.

The books of Ezra and Nehemiah, together with the prophets Haggai, Zechariah, and Malachi, tell us of some first steps in the right direction. Slowly, a number of Jews returned to Judah and began to rebuild both the city and the temple. This is the temple that stood in Jesus' day, though King Herod gives it a bit of renovation in between. In a very small way, therefore, we have a people in God's paradise land. But there is no king, and perhaps most significantly, God's presence never returns to the temple. This return from exile is certainly not the fulfillment of God's covenant promises. God's plans are much bigger.

New . . .

The word "new" can be a bit misleading. Take two examples: "I'm going to build a new house," and "He's become a new man since he married." In the first example, new means "never existed before." In the second, it has more the sense of "renewed" or "dramatically changed for the better." It is in this second sense that the new covenant is "new." It is a not a completely new creation unrelated to what came before. One of the longest sections on this new covenant comes in the book of Ezekiel, especially chapters 34–37. There, we see what the new covenant will bring about, and the categories and blessings are rather familiar:

People

"I will multiply . . . man and beast, and they shall multiply and be fruitful" (Ezekiel 36:11). Later, God makes Ezekiel take a stick and write "Judah" on it. Then he takes another stick and writes "Israel" on it. These two sticks, representing the two kingdoms, are bound together in a prophetic act, signifying that when the new covenant arrives, the Samaritans will be reunited with the people of Judah (Ezekiel 37:15ff.).

Paradise

> And the land that was desolate shall be tilled, instead of being the desolation that it was in the sight of all who passed by. And they will say, "This land that was desolate has become like the garden of Eden, and the waste and desolate and ruined cities are now fortified and inhabited."
> (Ezekiel 36:34–35)

Israel will once again be a land of plenty, so fruitful it can be compared to the garden of Eden.

God's Presence

> And I will put my Spirit within you, and cause you to walk in my statutes and be careful to obey my rules. You shall dwell in the

land that I gave to your fathers, and you shall be my people, and
I will be your God.
(Ezekiel 36:27–28)

I will be your God—God renews his promise to be with his
people. There are hints already, though, that this time he will
dwell with them in a different way from before. During the
days of the old covenant, he had put his Spirit-glory cloud in
the tabernacle and temple. Now, it seems God is going to live
in his people, through his Spirit.

The Covenant King

"My servant David shall be king over them, and they shall all
have one shepherd. They shall walk in my rules and be careful
to obey my statutes . . . David my servant shall be their prince
for ever" (Ezekiel 37:24–25).

David is back as king, and this time it's for ever. Again, while
this is very much in line with the covenant with David, there
does seem to be a new twist. Notice that the king is also called
a shepherd. Earlier in Ezekiel, God has already given a long
speech about these shepherd-kings. On the whole, they've been
doing a duff job, so God announces, "I myself will be the
shepherd of my sheep, and I myself will make them lie down,
declares the Lord GOD" (Ezekiel 34:15). God will come as
Shepherd-King. But didn't he say that David was going to fill
that role? He did: "I will set over them one shepherd, my
servant David." One king only. And it's God. And David. But
one person. Beginning to get the picture?

Going Large

But what's so new? Haven't we heard similar promises before?
Is this just God with his paintbrush dipped in water desperately

trying to cover over the mess his earth has become? Not this time—this time there's going to be a difference. And, as it's the last covenant he's going to make, this edition needs to be the one that brings a complete end to the ravages of the fall. This new covenant is going to be it, for there will be no more stages to God's covenant history, no more editions published. It's time for the fireworks to explode and the symphony to reach its climax. And if the climax is going to be on anything like the scale we'd expect from God, we'll need to see an extension in both the reach and the power of this new covenant.

Reach

First, then, reach: God goes global. Given his plan was always about filling a paradise world with his people, the new covenant is going to have to extend far beyond ethnic Israel, and so it does. The prophets foresee a day when the nations will return to God, when he is worshipped by Irish, Iranian, and Inuit, as well as Israelite.[1] Then there's the land. Isaiah paints pictures of lions and lambs lying down together in peace, of babies and boa constrictors playing together: the whole of creation will be renewed and become the "place" of God's glory.[2]

Power

This final covenant will actually need to *achieve* something. If this is going to be the final act of the drama, it will have to fully cleanse us of sin, fully remove suffering, fully restore God's dwelling on earth. This new covenant is the one that will deliver on all its predecessors' promises. To achieve this, it must genuinely deal with the death sentence that has been hanging over God's people. So far, they have been forgiven on credit. Just as when you buy a new TV on a credit card, you initially pay nothing but acknowledge that one day the bill will have to be settled, so for centuries God's people have been doing when they trusted in his covenant gospel. But their sin still needs to be paid for. The new covenant will have to pick up the tab—or rather it will be established by the man who will.[3]

In short, as the prophets look ahead to the day of the new covenant, they lead us to believe that a great Savior will both remove the covenant curses and bring in the covenant blessings. This great moment is often referred to as the "day of the Lord."[4] As we scour the prophets, we discover that when that day arrives, it will truly be a case of paradise restored.

The King Comes

Have you ever been in an evangelism training session where you were asked to turn to your neighbor and explain the gospel? If so, did your answer run at all along the lines of: "Well, there was a guy called Hezron who was the father of Ram, and Ram had a son called Amminadab. Now when Amminadab grew up, he had a boy and called him Nahshon. Now you won't believe this, but Nahshon had a son too . . ."

I imagine not. But this is really just another way of asking whether you've ever wondered why Matthew begins his Gospel with a chapter's worth of genealogy? If you were writing an account of what you considered to be the best news in the world, would you really begin with all those names? Matthew clearly thought so. But then, Matthew understood the covenant.

In his opening sentence Matthew calls Jesus "Jesus Christ, the son of David, the son of Abraham." He'll go on to list another forty-two generations, but wants to draw his readers' attention to Abraham and David in particular. Why? Because Abraham and David were the two Old Testament figures who received the covenant from God. Abraham was given the initial publication, setting out the blessings of people, paradise, and God's presence. Under David, the position of covenant king was added. Each was told the promises would be passed on to their own flesh and blood, specifically one "offspring." With Jesus, that one Offspring has arrived on earth to claim his inheritance.

Mark doesn't bother with a genealogy: he dives right in, telling us Jesus is the Christ, the rightful heir to David's throne. He then sets about demonstrating Jesus' authority over evil spirits, disease, sin, even death, giving us a taste of life under the covenant King.

Luke makes sure we don't miss the size of the inheritance coming Jesus' way. Tracing Jesus' ancestry right the way back to Adam, he is keen to portray Jesus as the ultimate faithful man, the King not just of Israel, but of all creation. So, straight after the genealogy, for example, Luke tells the story of Jesus resisting Satan's temptations, a clear contrast with his first ancestor. Christ's tests are even similar to Adam's: Jesus is tempted to take food illegitimately, as was Adam. Jesus is tempted to test God's Word, Adam to ignore it: "In the day that you eat of it you shall surely die" (Genesis 2:17). Jesus is tempted to steal glory for himself, Adam to try to become like God. In the same ditches that Adam stumbled, Jesus remains sure-footed. He will inherit the covenant blessings that Adam lost.

John kicks off by identifying Jesus as the Word who was with God and who was God. While remaining fully God and losing none of his powers or attributes, God the Son becomes human as well, and in John's words "dwelt [literally, tabernacled] among us" (John 1:14). Here is a stunning phrase. While in the Old Testament, God dwelt on earth in the glory cloud that led the Israelites through the desert and settled in the Holy of Holies of the tabernacle, now that same presence of God is found in Jesus. John is unmistakably clear: "We have seen his glory." Matthew also draws our attention to the fact that Jesus will be called Immanuel, which means: "God with us." "I will be your God, and you will be my people" has been the recurring melody of the covenant. Jesus quite literally embodies this principle—he is God with us.

All four Gospels are therefore in agreement: Jesus is the fulfillment of the "good shepherd" prophecies of Ezekiel 34: David's flesh and blood, but also God himself. The King has come. It is time for the new covenant to be put into action, and all the promises of the previous editions to be heaped upon their true Owner.

The Kingdom Comes

But as it turns out, the timescale is going to be somewhat different from the impression we may have picked up from the prophets. Jesus turns what looked like a one-stage rescue into a three-act drama.

Before we look at how he does this, we need to complete the story of Israel. We get into all sorts of trouble reading the Gospels, if we forget that first and foremost they are the climax of the story of Israel begun right back in Genesis 12. One of the parables that makes this most clear is the parable of the tenants (Mark 12). Comparing the Jewish leaders to tenants in a vineyard (Israel), Jesus points out that they have consistently rejected and abused the messengers that God, the true owner of Israel, has sent them. Finally, therefore, God has sent his Son—but he too will be met with rejection and ultimately murder. Perhaps the most chilling words in the New Testament are found on the lips of Israel's leaders: "This is the heir. Come, let us kill him" (Mark 12:7). Jesus is looking the Pharisees in the eye and saying, "You know who I am. You're not making a mistake. You are willfully and deliberately going to kill me, God's own Son, just as your forefathers killed his prophets."

This is going to mean the end of Israel as God's special people; the curses of Sinai will fully fall, ending that era of covenant history. Several times, Jesus prophesies that Jerusalem will soon be destroyed, as indeed it was in AD 70 at the hands of the Roman general Titus. The temple is pulled down, never to be rebuilt, and the Jewish people scattered throughout the empire. Outside of the covenant context, we might wonder why Jesus goes on so much about the fate awaiting the temple. But, once we realize he is speaking as the final covenant messenger, heralding the fall of the curses from Sinai, suddenly it all makes sense: the end has finally come for Israel.

Of course, this doesn't mean that someone who is ethnically Jewish is barred from the gospel—far from it. Most of the early church were Jewish, led by twelve Jewish apostles. And, while the passage is somewhat debated, it seems to me that in Romans 11 Paul looks forward to a day when a great number of Jews will turn back to Jesus. But as we saw earlier, under the new covenant God is going global, so ethnicity alone is no part of covenant membership.

So where is Jesus' kingdom? And who are his subjects? If we believe the prophets, the coming of the Messiah ought to have meant the whole world being filled with his glory—people from every tribe and nation streaming to Jerusalem to worship him. But as I mentioned earlier, there's a twist. Instead of bringing in the kingdom all at once, Jesus initiates it with his death and resurrection, continues to build now through his Spirit, and will one day return to complete the job. This means that, while some of the blessings promised by the prophets have arrived, not all have. It's a little tricky simply to parcel them up into two neat categories, but essentially there are "now" and "not-yet" blessings. Or perhaps better, each of our categories of people, place, and presence have "now" and "not-yet" aspects. This is hugely important for understanding what life should be like for us in our era of the covenant story.

The Now

In terms of people, Jesus in his final commission sent the disciples to all nations. From the start, Christianity was a missionary movement, not restricted to one culture, race, or continent. This movement began with the first Gentile conversions in the book of Acts, and continues today as new peoples are reached by the gospel.

This extension in the diversity of people has consequences for the place of Jesus' rule. There is no longer one geographic country we could draw a line around and mark as "God's Country";[5] there is no "holy land." Jesus now rules not from Jerusalem in Israel, but from heaven, which Paul significantly calls "the Jerusalem above" (Galatians 4:26).[6] Together with Paul's reference to the church as "the Israel of God" (Galatians 6:16), this shows us that God has not put two sets of promises in place: an earthly, physical plan for ethnic Israel and a heavenly, spiritual one for the church. No, the promises to Abraham find fulfillment in the even greater blessings of the new covenant. It's not that the church has *replaced* Israel—rather, to use biblical imagery, non-Jewish outsiders like me are grafted into the Israelite tree. Or, to change the picture, we become Abraham's children by sharing his faith rather than his DNA. Has God therefore failed to keep his promise? Not at all. If I promised you a second-hand car for your birthday and instead gave you a Porsche, would you accuse me of breaking my word? God has given his faithful people far more than may at first have met the eye.

But returning to the "where" of Jesus' kingdom, for now there is no physical land. Amazingly, Paul can say that, if you're a Christian, you are already seated in heaven. The real you, if I can put it like that, is safely there seated with Christ. "Nonsense!" you say. "I live in Derby." Well, it might sound strange, but I sometimes ask people to imagine they are tied to the end of one of those huge elastic cords brave people use to bungee-jump off bridges. The anchor of the cord is in heaven. We run around getting on with life down here, but waiting for the day that God has appointed for the cord to twang and whizz us safely back to heaven where our real roots are.

What of the final category: God's presence? For now, we experience that presence through the Holy Spirit. We're going to return to the Spirit in a later chapter, so we'll simply note here that he lives within all Christians, as a comforter, guide, and helper, guaranteeing that we'll finish the race.

The "Not Yet"

But is that it? Is the situation we now live in the final stage of God's plan? Far from it: if we compare the Old Testament prophecies of the new covenant with the present reality, we can see there are still items remaining on Jesus' to-do list. Hence, the many promises in the New Testament that Jesus will one day return to complete the covenant plan.

One of the best-loved passages in the Bible gives us a glimpse of this final state:

> Then I saw a new heaven and a new earth, for the first heaven and the first earth had passed away, and the sea was no more.

And I saw the holy city, new Jerusalem, coming down out of heaven from God, prepared as a bride adorned for her husband. And I heard a loud voice from the throne saying, "Behold, the dwelling place of God is with man. He will dwell with them, and they will be his people, and God himself will be with them as their God. He will wipe away every tear from their eyes, and death shall be no more, neither shall there be mourning, nor crying, nor pain any more, for the former things have passed away."

And he who was seated on the throne said, "Behold, I am making all things new." Also he said, "Write this down, for these words are trustworthy and true."

(Revelation 21:1–5)

Picturing a day in the future, when Christ has returned to bring his kingdom to completion, John takes us one last time through our now-familiar categories.

The paradise garden that began our story has become an entire universe. The whole earth is renewed. God's covenant people are not destined to spend eternity floating around on clouds, strumming harps. We will live in a physical paradise, complete with mountains, oceans, elephants, hedgehogs, heathland, lagoons, forests, and waterfalls. It will be even more beautiful than the first creation, while also no doubt containing many similarities. I imagine the Caribbean islands will be there, the Asian steppe, the plains of Africa. It is a new *earth* after all. The place the Bible calls heaven is therefore not our final destination—heaven is in fact more like the universe's best-ever waiting room, where Christians who die now live until Jesus returns. It's free from sin and suffering, but it isn't the physical resurrected universe. On the day Jesus returns, heaven and earth will finally be reunited.

The King's people will also be there. They are represented in Revelation 21 by the bride. Throughout the Bible, God uses the picture of marriage to teach us about his relationship with his people. The covenant does not create a cold legal relationship, obliging God to forgive us in the kind of begrudging way a toddler forgives his little sister on Mother's orders. No, covenant creates an even more intimate relationship between God and his people than marriage does between husband and wife. Here in the penultimate chapter of the Bible, the wedding day finally arrives. The new earth will be filled with people of all tribes, tongues, and nations, gathered round the throne to worship God. In fact, while we're mentioning worship, it might be worth pointing out that the Bible uses the word in both a narrow and a broad sense. Narrow is the one we are perhaps most used to: declaring praise to God directly. But more broadly, worship also refers to living our whole lives in a way that honors him. Both types of worship will presumably continue for eternity. Remember the cultural mandate back in Genesis 1 where God commanded men and women to develop and rule the earth? This will surely continue in the new earth.[7] We will continue to explore, to make music, invent machines, play sports, eat, drink, generally enjoy all the things that were a part of God's plan from the outset. Elsewhere, we learn we will have new bodies, resurrection bodies like Jesus' body. Our destiny is not to float like ghosts, but to run like Olympians. When we thought about this at church recently, my friend Reuben suggested we should start publishing lists of 101 things to do *after* you die, rather than before!

This time though, there will be no danger of the plan going wrong. For a start, we are told there will be no more death, pain, or sickness. Sin will not be a possibility. While some of the imagery of Revelation 21–22 may remind us of the garden of Eden, we are not just back at the beginning of the story again. No, Jesus the second Adam has passed the test, earned the covenant blessings, and ensured that they will not be taken away again.

Finally, God will come to be present with his covenant people in a special way. I'm not sure that we can guess exactly what it means for the "dwelling of God to be with man," but we can certainly be confident it's going to be good: in fact, good isn't the half of it. Stunning as the new earth will be, joyful as we will be to be reunited with old friends, the greatest reward of the gospel will be seeing God himself.

All these blessings are in the "not-yet" category. We need patience. Physical healing will come, but it is not promised yet. Eternal happiness will come, but not fully yet. Complete victory over sin will arrive, but again not yet. If we get confused and think these blessings should all be here now, we're either likely to get very angry with God for not keeping his promises or very down on ourselves for not doing enough to earn them. On the other hand, recovering the covenant timetable will help us live in patient, but eager, expectation.

The Sword Falls

If we're going to deal honestly and straightforwardly with the final day of covenant blessing though, we have to acknowledge fearfully that this is also the day when the curses fall for the final time: "But as for the cowardly, the faithless, the detestable, as for murderers, the sexually immoral, sorcerers, idolaters, and all liars, their portion will be in the lake that burns with fire and sulphur, which is the second death" (Revelation 21:8).

In breaking the covenant of works, Adam was cast from God's paradise. Those who broke the covenant of grace under Abraham were to be cut off from their people. Under Moses, covenant-breaking resulted in exile or death. Here, covenant-breakers are consigned to an eternity of suffering in hell. The second death has arrived. Earlier, in Revelation 19, Satan himself has been cast into the fiery lake. Satan doesn't rule hell but is imprisoned there. Jesus rules hell. In Revelation 14:10–11, we read that a person who rejects Jesus as their covenant King

> will drink the wine of God's wrath, poured full strength into the cup of his anger, and he will be tormented with fire and sulphur in the presence of the holy angels and in the presence of the Lamb. And the smoke of their torment goes up for ever and ever, and they have no rest, day or night.

Jesus will defeat his enemies. He either conquers them through the gospel so they become his friends or punishes them with the terrors of hell. This short passage teaches us three things about hell. First, it is eternal: it never comes to an end. Second, people are conscious in hell. They do not go to sleep, or cease to exist. And third, it is torment. While I'm not sure that we're meant to interpret the lake of sulphur strictly literally, we can be sure that the reality is no less terrifying.

Hell is eternal, conscious torment. There is no getting out, no second chance. Even to talk of a second chance is to slander God. We have had endless chances on earth. George Whitefield wrote that "The terror of hell is to burn like coals for thousands and thousands of ages only to realize at the end of them that they are no closer to getting out than at the beginning." It is the exact opposite of those wonderful lines from "Amazing Grace":

> When we've been there ten thousand years,
>> bright shining like the sun,
> we've no less days to sing God's praise,
>> than when we first begun.[8]

We are meant to read these passages from Revelation and shudder. They should drive us to Christ as the only refuge, and fill us with praise for the rescue he offers. They should also fill us with tears, prayers, and passion for those still rebelling.

The Starter's Pistol

So, the new covenant has begun, but not yet been fulfilled. Already, we have the pouring out of the Holy Spirit, the spread of the gospel to all nations, the movement from a focus on Israel and Jerusalem to the church of Jew and Gentile scattered across the earth. For now, therefore, the covenant conditions remain on offer. To enter the kingdom, every man, woman, and child must repent and believe the good news (Mark 1:15): faith, as ever, is the only condition of the gospel.

In the "not-yet" category, the new earth remains to be revealed, we still don't have resurrection bodies, and Jesus hasn't returned to claim his kingdom.

But what brought about the beginning of this final stage of covenant history? It was the sacrifice of the Son of God, offering himself in place of his people to remove the

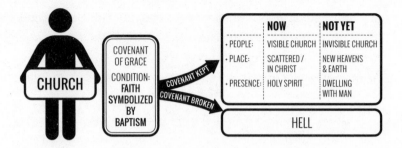

covenant curses from them. During his last night on earth, while eating with the disciples, Jesus took a cup of wine and said, "This cup is the new covenant in my blood, which is poured out for you" (Luke 22:20 NIV). To understand Jesus' words, and begin to link the covenant story to the covenant gospel, we need to turn our attention to one last covenant.

THE COVENANT
OF REDEMPTION

An Unresolved Mystery

Have you ever been out-thought by a three-year-old? It's not often that it happens, particularly in the world of theology, but my friend Tim's son had him on toast the other day. Tim had just found little Josh committing some toddler-level misdemeanor. It was a fair cop, and Josh was caught red-handed. But like the best criminal masterminds, Josh already had his escape route planned. According to Tim, the conversation went something along the lines of:

Josh: "Do you remember our Bible story last night, Daddy?"

Tim: "Er, yes."

Josh: "Where you said God had forgotten all my sin and all your sin and would never punish us for it again?"

Tim (beginning to sense the danger): "Well, yes, but . . ."

Josh: "Don't you think it would be better if you did the same and just forgot about this?"

And away Josh walked, no doubt to a lucrative career in law in years to come.

Now, here's the question: who do you think had best grounds to think God would be on their side? Tim could rightly demand justice for the crimes committed. Josh, on the other hand, appealed to the mercy and forgiveness that is promised in the gospel. Both have a legitimate claim on a God who describes himself as both light and love. After all, he promises justice for the oppressed, but also mercy for sinners.

What Tim and Josh were experiencing, albeit in a very small way, was a tension between the two covenants we've so far examined. According to the first covenant, the covenant of works, Adam and all human beings after him are covenant-breakers. We simply must die; there is no way around it. Yet the covenant of grace, in each of its successive editions, has promised great blessings to God's people. Abraham received these blessings. So did Moses. And David. And Isaiah. And Daniel. And countless other nameless Israelites and Christians. What was the condition? Simply that they trusted God as Savior and took him as their Lord.

But how come? Abraham wasn't righteous. He sinned, and sinned big. On one occasion, he even prostituted his wife to Pharaoh. Then, for good measure, he did it again a few years later with the Gentile king Abimilech. How can simply having faith mean that Abraham gets away scot-free? How can someone who is under the curse of the covenant of works instead inherit the blessings of the covenant of grace?

This is a very real question: will the fact that you or I have faith in Christ be enough to save us? Can we be sure?

A Very Biblical Mystery

This tension between the covenant of works and the covenant of grace is not some problem imposed on the Bible by covenant theologians. The puzzle comes right from the mouth of God:

> The Lord passed before [Moses] and proclaimed, "The Lord, the Lord, a God merciful and gracious, slow to anger, and abounding in steadfast love and faithfulness, keeping steadfast love for thousands, forgiving iniquity and transgression and sin, but who will by no means clear the guilty."
> (Exodus 34:6–7)

"Merciful and gracious . . . forgiving iniquity and transgression": good, gospel news. "By no means clearing the guilty": there's the problem. If you're guilty, you must be punished. I wonder if we Christians sometimes miss this, used as we are to the idea of God being merciful. God cannot just arbitrarily decide to let a bunch of people off their sin. That would be to deny both his character and his covenant promise that all who sin must die. Forgiveness cannot come about by God closing his eyes and allowing a chosen few to sneak over the back wall into heaven.

Interestingly, God gives this revelation to Moses after Moses had asked to "see" God's glory. Rather than putting on a spectacular firework display, God speaks of covenant tension. Whatever the answer to the problem, God has announced it will be the greatest revelation of his glory. Get this: if you want to see God at his most glorious, you will have to watch him find a way of *both* justly punishing every sinner, while also demonstrating mercy and forgiveness. As J. I. Packer promised right back in chapter 1, rediscovering the covenants will give us a clearer window into the very character of God.

Let's clarify one thing first. Many Christians think the answer to the dilemma is obvious: they are happy to say God can forgive us "because we have faith" and leave it pretty much at that. But to be blunt, faith itself never saved anyone. Not in the Old Testament, not in the New, and not now. Believing that God exists or that Jesus is God or that he came back from the dead in and of itself can do nothing much for you—after all, the devil believes just as much. The fact remains, you've still broken the covenant of works and are still due to face God as an enemy. If all we had was faith, we'd be in a whole host of trouble. Faith can't save you.

But Jesus can save us, and he does so through the last of the Bible's covenants: the covenant of redemption.

The Covenant of Redemption

Here, we need to leave the story of the covenant and travel outside of time itself to eavesdrop on a conversation between God the Father and God the Son. (You'll understand, of course, that this is just a human way of putting it.) Jesus lets us know that he and his Father made an arrangement. Theologians have often called it "the covenant of redemption." As this name suggests, it was a plan to redeem, or save, humanity. Evidence of this covenant pops up every time we get a glimpse of the Father and Son talking to each other, or when Jesus reveals a promise his Father made to him. One such time is John 17:

> When Jesus had spoken these words, he lifted up his eyes to heaven, and said, "Father, the hour has come; glorify your Son that the Son may glorify you, since you have given him authority over all flesh, to give eternal life to all whom you have given him. And this is eternal life, that they know you the only true God, and Jesus Christ whom you have sent. I glorified you on earth, having accomplished the work that you gave me to do. And now, Father,

glorify me in your own presence with the glory that I had with you before the world existed."
(John 17:1–5)

OK, I know the word covenant isn't actually used here. But remember the simplest definition: **a covenant is a conditional promise**. Each element is found in the arrangement between God the Father and God the Son (and indeed God the Spirit, as we'll discover later). So we see:

1. *The Condition*
Jesus says that there is a "work that you [the Father] gave me to do." When did this job assigning happen? Certainly, before Jesus came to earth, as part of the work was the very task of becoming human and entering our world. Here is a covenant that takes us back to eternity past, and into the heart of the Trinity. The Father sends; the Son is sent.

And why did they engage upon this mission? In brief, Jesus speaks of his work as having two aims. First, he came in order to "glorify God on earth," not to *make* God glorious: clearly, God is already as full of glory as he could possibly be. Rather, Jesus' mission was to spread the news of that glory from heaven, where it is rightfully acknowledged, to earth, where it is routinely ignored. If I drive to a new town and spend the afternoon telling everyone how beautiful my wife is, I am not making her more beautiful, but "beautifying" her in a new place.

Jesus has a second task: "to give eternal life to all [the Father has] given him." This, in fact, is how he achieves his first goal. By moving Adam's offspring from death to life, he changes them from being people who hate God to people who now love and worship him.

2. The Promise

In return for this work, Jesus is rewarded, as we'd expect from a covenant; appointed as King over all humanity, or "all flesh" as he puts it; and also given a more specific people to rule over. Then, having all but completed his work, he claims his final reward, to spend eternity in glory, in his Father's presence.

Do you see the covenant pattern emerging? Two "people," a task set, a condition met, a reward given.

All of which is good news for Jesus, but it doesn't answer our big question: how can millions and millions of sinners justly enter paradise with him? To return to our earlier illustration, is Jesus simply smuggling his people illegitimately over the back wall, into a heaven we have no right to enter?

Rewriting History

To get to the bottom of this mystery, we need to look more closely at how Jesus saves his people and focus on the conditions of this covenant.

John 17 doesn't give all the detail, but we learn from elsewhere in the Bible that *from Jesus' point of view, the covenant of redemption is essentially the covenant of works.* It's as if God sets Jesus back at the beginning of our covenant story and invites him to have another go. That's why Jesus is sometimes called the "last Adam." Adam One messed things up, so Adam Two came to the rescue. This is nicely captured in John Newman's hymn: "Praise to the Holiest in the Height":

> O loving wisdom of our God!
> When all was sin and shame,
> A second Adam to the fight
> And to the rescue came.[1]

Paul makes exactly this point in Romans 5:

> Therefore, as one trespass led to condemnation for all men, so one act of righteousness leads to justification and life for all men. For as by the one man's disobedience the many were made sinners, so by the one man's obedience the many will be made righteous. (Romans 5:18–19)

Like Adam, Jesus represents his people. Except this time, it is not guilt, grime, and the grave that flow to his people, but righteousness, renewal, and resurrection. In order for this to happen though, Jesus is going to have a much harder time than Adam. After all, Adam simply had to obey while living in paradise. But once he'd disobeyed and brought down the curses, whoever was going to undo his work must both remove the curse and start all over again to earn the blessing.

If you'll excuse a slightly daft illustration to clarify this double nature of Jesus' work, imagine God had put Adam in a classroom rather than a garden. Then, instead of telling him to fill the earth and avoid the forbidden fruit, picture God handing Adam a page of long multiplications. Eternal life rested on him getting 100% right. Adam effectively took the pen, ignored the sums, and instead scrawled a bunch of abusive messages across the page. God responds by failing Adam and handing him a detention. When Jesus enters the room to put things right, he needs to do two things: deal with the punishment *and* fill in the right answers.

There are therefore two aspects to Jesus' saving work. Through the covenant of redemption Christ takes on himself the curse of the covenant of works. But he also needs to fulfill its terms and earn its blessings. Traditionally, these have been known respectively as his passive and active obedience.

Active and passive are here being used in a slightly old-fashioned sense. Jesus' passive obedience is his whole work of removing the curse, coming under all its penalties in our place. In the classroom illustration, this is Jesus taking the detention for Adam. Evangelicals tend to be strong on identifying this feature of our salvation.

Where we're perhaps less strong is on remembering Jesus' active obedience. This is what Jesus does positively to fulfill the covenant of works; in other words, his perfect, spotless, and wholehearted obedience to his Father—even more impressive in the midst of a sin-ravaged world. To go back to the classroom, this is Jesus getting the answers right and earning the reward.

So, Christ doesn't just undo the mess that Adam gets us into. If he only removed the effects of Adam's fall (passive obedience), then we'd be back to square one—Jesus has wound the clock back, returned us to Eden, and said, "Have another go"; he has wiped the page clear and left us with the sums. That's absolutely the last thing we need, for we'd surely mess up as quickly as Adam did and soon find ourselves in the same trouble. No, Jesus' rescue is the whole package: full-fat salvation. He not only removes the damage; he also ensures it won't happen again. This is hugely exciting and, once we get our heads around it, makes salvation even more amazing!

The Give-and-Take Savior

Let's focus on Jesus' work of giving and taking: taking our curses and giving his blessings. We'll look at each of the three problems we received from the first Adam: the grave, guilt, and our grimy hearts. And we'll see the second Adam answer in turn with gifts of resurrection, righteousness, and renewal.

1. The Grave

Jesus Takes: The Grave

The wages of sin is death. Jesus never sinned, so why should he have to die? Well, whereas Adam in Eden was covenant king of a race of (at that stage theoretically) sinless people, Christ comes and unites himself to unrighteous covenant-breakers. By doing so, he's uniting himself to their death penalty and he dies in union with his people.

This is why it was essential for Jesus to be fully human. Throughout the Old Testament, believers would sacrifice animals to atone for their sin. But, as the author of Hebrews teaches us, this could never be a real solution:

> For it is impossible for the blood of bulls and goats to take away sins. Consequently, when Christ came into the world, he said,
>
> "Sacrifices and offerings you have not desired,
>   but a body have you prepared for me;
> in burnt offerings and sin offerings
>   you have taken no pleasure.
> Then I said, 'Behold, I have come to do your will, O God,
>   as it is written of me in the scroll of the book.'"
> (Hebrews 10:4–7)

Only humans can pay the price for human sin. That's why Jesus became a man, why God "prepared a body" for him. A second Adam took flesh and became part of the race of sinners. No angel could die for us. God himself could not die for us. Only the God-*man* could stand in our place.

This is why Paul can write, "Christ redeemed us from the curse of the law by becoming a curse for us—for it is written,

'Cursed is everyone who is hanged on a tree' " (Galatians 3:13).
When Jesus died, he did so bearing the covenant curse. His
crown of thorns reminds us of the first time the curses were
pronounced, right back in Genesis 3, where thorns on the earth
became a symbol of God's curses. When Jesus cries, "My God,
my God, why have you forsaken me?" (Matthew 27:46), he is
experiencing the curse of being cut off from his Father's
presence to bless him: being cut off has been the threat
right through our covenant story. He is, in other words, going
through hell on the cross, in place of his people. All God's
wrath rains down on him, because he is representing them.
This is why Jesus refers to his blood as "blood of the covenant . . .
poured out . . . for the forgiveness of sins" (Matthew 26:28).
This blood pays the penalty for the breaking of the covenant
of works.

Jesus Gives: Resurrection
Jesus also gives us resurrection life. Nowhere is this theme
better explored than in 1 Corinthians 15. Comparing the bodies
we inherited from Adam to bodies we will one day inherit from
Jesus, Paul says, "Just as we have borne the image of the man
of dust, we shall also bear the image of the man of heaven"
(1 Corinthians 15:49).

What will this resurrection life be like? What is a resurrection body? After telling the Corinthians that only a fool
would pretend to know the full answer, Paul goes on to give
them some idea:

> So is it with the resurrection of the dead. What is sown
> is perishable; what is raised is imperishable. It is sown in
> dishonor; it is raised in glory. It is sown in weakness;
> it is raised in power. It is sown a natural body; it is raised a

spiritual body. If there is a natural body, there is also a spiritual body.

(1 Corinthians 15:42–44)

The resurrection bodies Jesus earns for us will never wither or fade. They will be "spiritual" not in the sense of "not physical," but rather "full of the Spirit and fit for heaven." In short, they will be far more glorious even than Adam's original sinless body.

2. Guilt

Jesus Takes: Our Guilt

As he has taken the curse in place of his people, their guilty status before God can now change. No longer are they sinners bearing the legal guilt of being in Adam.

The Bible often uses the picture of financial debt to teach us about sin. When we're forgiven, our debt is wiped away. However filthy your sin, however ashamed you are, however badly you've hurt God or a fellow human being, it has been wiped away.

Jesus Gives: His Righteousness

And the covenant gospel is even better news than that. Because we are united with Jesus, his record now becomes ours.

When I was a student, I would end the academic year heavily overdrawn, usually by £1,500, the most I was allowed by my bank to get into debt. I'd then spend the summer working. One particularly pleasant year, I worked at a cake factory. It might sound good, but the smell of thousands of cream éclairs at 5am was enough to put you off cake for life (nearly). Anyway, I'd work for three months, at about £500 a month, and by the end of the "holidays," I'd be ready to go back to university with a bank balance of . . . zero. Ouch! All that work, and I was just back to scratch. What I actually needed was more than this: I needed a millionaire long-lost uncle to transfer some of his fortune into my account!

This, in fact, is what Jesus has done for us. Rather than our "spiritual accounts" being wiped free of debt and just returned to zero, they are given infinite credit. The Bible calls this "justification" or being counted as righteous. Romans 5:18–19 reminds us that through Adam's sin we became guilty. It also tell us that, through Jesus' obedience and death, our status becomes "righteous" or "justified." When God looks on us now, in Christ, he sees people who are fully obedient, who have loved the Lord with all our hearts, who have never been selfish, never been sexually impure, always relied on God in prayer—in short, he sees Jesus the covenant Keeper!

3. Grime

Jesus Takes: Our Grime
Remember that, as well as the legal status of "guilty," we also received corrupt, grimy natures from Adam. Like bowling balls, we have a natural swerve away from obedience and toward sin. Paul says that we are by nature "slaves to sin," unable to break free. Indeed, we *love* sinning and have no desire to stop.

Until, that is, Jesus comes to rescue us. When we died with Jesus, the power of sin over us was killed too. "For one who has died has been set free from sin" (Romans 6:7). We no longer have to sin: the chains have been broken, and we can walk free from the tyranny. Here, the focus is on Jesus overcoming the power of sin in our day-to-day lives. He removes our hearts of stone, with their determination to lead grubby, sinful lives.

Jesus Gives: Renewal

But it's not just that we are now able to resist sin if we choose to, equivalent to returning us to the garden and telling us to have another go. Remember when Jesus takes a curse away, he always gives a blessing in its place? This time, he gives us renewed hearts that positively want to obey him.

To return to the bowling ball illustration, we now swerve toward holiness. Until we die or Jesus returns, this is an incomplete transformation. We are, sadly, still able to fall into sin. But because he has given us the gift of the Holy Spirit, the remaining sin in us will not win. Jesus' Spirit is far more powerful. One day, he will transform us fully and finally. In the new heavens and new earth we will have no desire to sin, but will delight in living holy, loving lives.

Paul says of the transformation, "But thanks be to God, that you who were once slaves of sin have become obedient from the heart to the standard of teaching to which you were committed, and, having been set free from sin, have become slaves of righteousness" (Romans 6:17–18). "Obedient from the heart": Christ's people have new natures and renewed hearts that will lead to lives of ever-increasing degrees of holiness. We are even "slaves of righteousness," ultimately not able to resist living holy lives!

I hope you can now grasp how exciting it is to see the double work of Jesus, active and passive: not just taking our curses and returning us to Eden, but giving all we need to join him in a resurrected world.

Back to the Story

How does all this fit with the covenant story earlier? What is the relationship between the covenant of redemption and the covenant of grace? After all, it is the covenant of grace that is revealed in history, made with human beings like us. How do all the promises of a people, paradise, and his presence fit into Jesus' rescue?

The Offspring

Speaking of the covenant of grace, Paul says, "Now the promises were made to Abraham and to his offspring. It does not say, 'And to offsprings,' referring to many, but referring to one, 'And to your offspring,' who is Christ" (Galatians 3:16).

Paul is quoting Genesis 13:15 and Genesis 17:8, both of which tell of God promising the paradise land to Abraham and his offspring. Paul's point is that, *first and foremost*, "offspring" was meant to refer not to all Abraham's physical children (the Jews) or all his spiritual children (anyone who believes), but to one man—Jesus. And God would give Jesus the covenant blessings of paradise, a people, and his presence.

This should now make sense: only Jesus earned them, after all, fulfilling the conditions of the covenants of redemption and works (the same thing from his point of view, as we've just seen). Perhaps you noticed from his prayer in John 17 that Jesus' reward for this covenant obedience was a people to rule over in God's presence? All the threads are beginning to come together to reveal the brilliant tapestry of God's plan. Jesus actually receives the blessings that Abraham, David, and company passed on down the generations, until their true Offspring arrived. They didn't deserve them, but Jesus did.

But we're not quite done yet. A few verses later Paul goes on to say, "And if you are Christ's, then you are Abraham's offspring, heirs according to promise" (Galatians 3:29). In a secondary sense, everyone who believes the gospel promises is Abraham's offspring. Is Paul contradicting what he said just a few verses earlier, that "offspring" meant Jesus? No, because of the union between Christ and his people. In the covenant of redemption, Jesus agreed that he would bind himself to his people, so the two become one.

One of the best Bible pictures of this is marriage. When Adam and Eve marry, we are told they become "one flesh." In fact, Adam sings that Eve is "bone of my bones and flesh of my flesh" (Genesis 2:23). Years later, Paul says that, mysteriously, this is the relationship between Christ and his church. He's not just looking around for an interesting way to say Jesus loves us lots and lots. No, through a mystical union that we'll explore in future chapters, we are one flesh with Jesus, bone of his bones and flesh of his flesh. Everything that happens to him therefore happens to us.

So, if we are united to him, we receive what he receives—a place in the paradise of God, among the people of God, in the presence of God. What we need is to be connected to Jesus. From our end, that connection is faith: the condition of the covenant of grace. If we keep this condition and trust in Jesus, we are immediately attached to the faithful covenant King together with all the blessings he enjoys.

This is huge. The story of the Bible is constantly emphasizing the three *p's*. When we arrive at some of the New Testament letters, we find more emphasis on the give-and-take rescue of Jesus: grave, guilt, and grime taken, resurrection, righteousness, and renewed hearts given. Which is the "real" gospel? How do story and salvation fit together?

In the covenant of redemption. God gives Jesus all the blessings of the story: he is the end to which the whole story has been driving. But the covenant of redemption is also the means by which Jesus can deal with our spiritual problems.

This is why at the last supper Jesus called his blood "covenant blood." He is teaching us that at the cross he won not just forgiveness, but therefore also a place among God's people in the future paradise world. He is connecting story and salvation. So, salvation is all about union with Christ our covenant King. John Calvin recognizes as much:

> We must now see in what way we become possessed of the blessings which God has bestowed on his only-begotten Son, not for private use, but to enrich the poor and needy. And the first thing to be attended to is, that so long as we are without Christ and separated from him, nothing which he suffered and did for the salvation of the human race is of the least benefit to us . . . all which he possesses being, as I have said, nothing to us until we become one with him.[2]

The Mystery Solved

We started this chapter by looking at the tension between God's promise to forgive and his promise that he would not clear the guilty. We're now beginning to see how both of these can be true. The covenant of redemption that we've been examining holds the key. In it, Jesus and his people become as closely united as your hand is to your arm. When Jesus is punished, his people are punished: we are one flesh and bone after all. God therefore does not just forget our sin or pretend it doesn't matter. No, he punishes it; he punishes us. Abraham *is* punished for prostituting Sarah. Noah *is* punished for getting drunk. David *is* punished for seducing and stealing Bathsheba. But thankfully, they and we are punished in union with Christ, so we don't experience the curse ourselves. That means God can then forgive those for whom Christ died. As a song I learned at summer camp around the time I was converted says,

At the cross of Jesus, pardon is complete,
Love and justice mingle, truth and mercy meet.
Though my sins condemn me, Jesus died instead;
There is full forgiveness, in the blood he shed.[3]

God is just: he punishes sin as he must. God is forgiving: he punishes sin in his own Son, so together they can forgive his people. This is why the cross is the place where God most clearly shows his glory. When Moses prayed that he would see God's glory, God *proclaimed* that he would punish the guilty and also forgive them. When Jesus prayed that God would glorify himself, what happened? The next day he was crucified, and as he hung there, the guilty were punished and forgiven, all in the same action. Only a glorious God could achieve such a great salvation!

9

COVENANT SALVATION

REMEMBER J. I. PACKER'S observation that it is the covenants that link the Bible's story to the Bible's salvation? Having traced that story, we've seen two figures come to the fore, as the diagram below demonstrates:

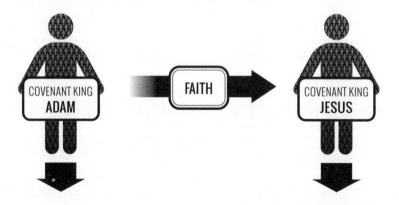

Clearly, the priority for every human being is to move from Adam to Christ. But how does the transfer happen? The first answer we have seen already: through the covenant of grace. If we repent and believe God's good news of a rescuer-king, we are united to Jesus and therefore to his blessings.

But if we leave it there, a problem remains. If you were to ask the question: "Why does Anna end up in heaven and Barney not?", the answer would be "Because Anna believes." That's true as far as it goes. But we've not gone as deep into the doctrine of grace as God would have us go.

Saved by Grace. Oh, And . . .

Most Christians are clear that we are saved by grace. To be saved by grace is simply to be saved by God. Where we are perhaps less confident is in realizing that we are saved by grace *alone*, or, in other words, by God alone.

For years, my understanding of the gospel went something along the lines of: "Jesus has died for everyone's sins, but it doesn't work automatically. You need to choose to believe in him." I would certainly have said I believed in salvation by grace, possibly even grace alone. I sang "Amazing Grace," "In Christ Alone," and "To God Be the Glory" with a sincere heart. But underneath, I saw salvation as more of a cooperative effort. Jesus does the dying for us and offers us the gospel. We, out of our own free will, decide whether to accept it or not. He won't force us to believe, because, if he did, it wouldn't be loving or respectful of our free will.

Although I would never have put it like this, in reality I saw God as doing 95% of the work and then us needing to fill up the final 5% by believing the gospel message. God and Jesus did all the work getting the lifeboat in place, without which I'd never be saved. But I had to climb in. Or, in terms of our diagrams above, it was my job to transfer myself from Adam to Christ, which I did by having faith.

I was wrong. There are at least three problems that arise from this view of salvation. The first is pastoral: it robs us of assurance, of confidence we'll be saved. If it was me who put myself "in Christ," then presumably I can put myself back into Adam again? What happens if I stop believing? I can never know for certain that I'll make it to heaven until I'm dead, by which time it's too late to do anything about it anyway.

The second problem is what we might call "theological": this cooperation view robs God of glory. Salvation is no longer by God alone. The credit for me ending up in heaven will be shared. Yes, I'll thank God for sending Jesus, I'll praise Jesus for dying for me, and in a quiet moment I'd be entitled to give myself a pat on the back for realizing the whole thing was true. Well done God, well done Jesus, well done Jonty.

The third problem is practical. If the final 5% of someone becoming a Christian rests in their hands, then what's the point in praying for them? I can sit and pray, "Father God, I'd love for Jemima to become a Christian. Please soften her heart so that she follows Jesus," but God is going to have to say back, "Yup, me too. I'd love her to worship me. But her heart is her heart, beyond my reach. There's not much I can do about it." Now, let me quickly say that those who do hold to this cooperation view of salvation do in reality pray for their friends to be converted. My point is that their practice is (thankfully) inconsistent with their belief.

So, what does move us from Adam to Christ? How does this covenant story help us understand our salvation? We'll see that each of the three persons of the Trinity plays their part in ensuring the transfer is truly by God alone. And each of their actions gives a different angle on the love of God poured out on his people.

1. Unconditional Love: The Father Chooses a People

The first point at which you were moved from Adam to Christ was technically not a point in time at all.

> [God] chose us in him before the foundation of the world, that we should be holy and blameless before him. In love he predestined us for adoption as sons through Jesus Christ, according to the purpose of his will, to the praise of his glorious grace, with which he has blessed us in the Beloved.
> (Ephesians 1:4–6)

It is God who chooses who will become his sons and daughters. This "election" or "predestination" happened not just before we were born, but before the universe was born even. Notice that this choosing happens "in him" (Jesus). God decided for himself who would be moved from Adam to Christ long before Adam had even fallen.

Sometimes, people try to pretend all this election stuff is just an invention of the apostle Paul. But John can divide humankind into two categories of people: those whose names were or weren't "written before the foundation of the world in the book of life of the Lamb who was slain" (Revelation 13:8). In Acts, Luke ends his account of an evangelistic meeting with: "as many as were appointed to eternal life believed" (Acts 13:48). Jesus himself tells the disciples, "You did not choose me, but I chose you," and preaches to the crowds that "No one can come to me unless the Father who sent me draws him" (John 15:16; 6:44). This is also why he referred so often to "those the Father has given me" (see John 6:37; 10:29).

God's choosing of people is entirely unconditional, not based on anything good in them. It is not, for example, like children picking football teams in the playground, where the sporty kids get picked first, and the less coordinated ones are left out on the sidelines. There is nothing special about those chosen that marks them out; they have no reason to feel superior to those not chosen.

Nor does God look down the centuries, see who will choose him, and then choose them himself too. Sometimes, people try and evade the Bible's clear teaching on election by shifting the ultimate decision from God to human beings. But if God is simply recognizing and then echoing our choice, in what sense can he be said to be choosing himself? All this does is put us back in the mess of having salvation being 95% God and 5% human again. It opens up the pastoral, theological, and practical problems mentioned above. It also flatly contradicts the Bible's teaching: "[God] saved us and called us to a holy calling, not because of our works but because of his own purpose and grace, which he gave us in Christ Jesus before the ages began" (2 Timothy 1:9).

Election is not based on our works, nor on our having faith. Not that it's random either: sometimes Christians are so keen to protect the graciousness of God's choice that they almost portray him as shutting his eyes and reaching out blind to grab a bunch of people. God chooses us "because of his own purpose." We aren't told what that purpose is, but we are told it does exist. God does not play dice for your salvation.

So, the first step in moving you from Adam to Christ is God the Father choosing you. This reminds us that his love is utterly unconditional: if he chose you not just before you, but before the universe, existed, then you certainly did nothing to earn it. Why is this such good news? Because, if we did nothing to earn it, we are therefore in no danger of "un-earning" it. Salvation is by grace alone and by God alone, an entirely unconditional love that rescues us.

2. Personal Love: The Son Dies for His People

God's love is also personal. In a sense, we've seen this already: the Father chooses real people. And Jesus dies for them: "I am the good shepherd. The good shepherd lays down his life for the sheep" (John 10:11). Here we come to the second "moment" you were moved from Adam to Christ. Jesus is mysteriously united to the covenant-breaking "sheep" the Father has given him. He therefore dies under their curse (as we saw in the last chapter). This means that Paul can say not just that Christ died for us, but also that "we died with Christ" (Romans 6:8; Colossians 2:20).

If this is right, then the answer to the question: "For whom did Jesus die?" is not: "Every single person who has ever lived," but: "Only those the Father chose." This may come as a shock to some of you, so let me explain further.

Jesus' Death Is Personal

When Jesus says he will lay his life down "for the sheep," who is he talking about?

> My sheep hear my voice, and I know them, and they follow me.
> I give them eternal life, and they will never perish, and no one
> will snatch them out of my hand. My Father, who has given them
> to me, is greater than all, and no one is able to snatch them out
> of the Father's hand.
> (John 10:27–29)

Sheep are people who are given to Jesus by the Father. In theory so far, this could mean everyone: perhaps the Father gave absolutely every single person to Jesus? But then we read that sheep have eternal life: that they will arrive safely in heaven, through all the trials and temptations of this earthly life. We also learn that sheep follow Jesus and listen to him as their Master.

If we put these pieces together, we see that these sheep for whom Jesus died:

- Are given to Jesus by God the Father
- Will definitely go to heaven
- Follow Jesus

This cannot be a description of everyone, everywhere. No, "sheep" are those people who become Christians, the same group of people that the Father chooses, or those whose names he writes in the book of life. Jesus died to take the curse not for every single individual without exception, but for his church.

The great news here is that Jesus' death is personal. When he hung on the cross, he was dying for you, if you're a Christian. He was not dying "for sin" in some general sense. "Sin" doesn't exist as a thing in its own right. You can't detach sin from the sinner. So, when Jesus takes the punishment for sin, he takes the punishment for particular sinners, those given to him in the covenant of redemption. If you are someone who follows Jesus, you are a sheep. Jesus knows you now, and knew you when he was bearing your curse. This makes Jesus' love for you so much more personal, and is far sweeter news than the picture of Jesus dying for sin-in-general and then heading back to heaven to see what would happen next. And of course, it means Jesus wasn't dying for everyone: for the atonement to be personal, it has to be "particular."

Jesus' Death Is Powerful
When the angel appeared to Joseph, he told him to give Mary's son the name Jesus, "for he will save his people from their sins"

(Matthew 1:21). He *will*, not might, save his people. And the Bible is packed full of verses that talk about the cross, the place where salvation was achieved: "For Christ . . . died for sins, once and for all, the righteous for the unrighteous, that he might bring us to God" (1 Peter 3:18 RSV). Jesus' death does everything that needs doing in order for us to be "brought to God." As he died, Jesus cried, "It is finished" (John 19:30). Mission accomplished. Jesus did not cry out, "It's now a possibility!" He actually saved people; he didn't just make salvation an option for those who are spiritual or smart enough to believe. And if Jesus' death did the work to reconcile his people to God, clearly he can't have been dying for everyone without exception, or else everyone would be reconciled.

The fact that Jesus didn't die for every single human without exception came as a shock to me. As I said, it may be a shock to you too. Here are some points to ponder:

- Did Jesus die for Hitler's sin? If so, on what grounds can he refuse Hitler entry to heaven? God is just, so he cannot punish sin twice.
- We know that Jesus died for people like Abraham and Moses who lived before him but trusted God's covenant gospel without knowing all the details. They were therefore in heaven already, when Jesus died. But did Jesus die for the sins of those who lived before him and were already in hell by the time he was crucified?
- We've already seen that the Father chooses some, not all. We'll see in a minute that the Holy Spirit gives life to some people, not all. Would it make sense for Jesus to be the "odd one out"? Would he come and die for people *knowing* that his Father had not chosen them and that the Holy Spirit was not going to give them faith?

No, the three persons of the Trinity always work together: Jesus was not on a solo mission, going against the will of the Father and Spirit. If the Father and Spirit choose, so too does Jesus. As Charles Spurgeon once said, why should it be that we are happy to choose our own wives, but are unwilling that Christ be allowed the same privilege!

Sometimes, this doctrine is called "limited atonement." That's a terrible name, because it sounds as if the cross is somehow not quite as effective as it might have been. Instead, as I've tried to show above, this view of Jesus' death actually protects and even increases its powerful and personal nature. Many people therefore prefer the term "particular atonement," or "effective atonement." Call it what you like though, it does reduce the number of people for whom Jesus died.[1]

So, in case you're beginning to think this in some way undermines Jesus' work, remember that, if you want to argue that Jesus died for everyone without exception, you'll have to "limit" the cross too. Usually, this involves limiting the power of his death.[2] If he died for everyone, so the argument goes, and if we know not everyone is saved, then Jesus' death can't itself have saved anyone. You need to add something to Jesus' work in order to gain salvation. Jesus opened the door to heaven, but it's something else that actually gets you through. For Roman Catholics, it is the church and sacraments that move you through the door. For many non-Reformed evangelicals, it is believing the gospel that does the work. Both see Jesus' death as necessary, but not sufficient in and of itself, to save. This seems to me to be a far worse "limiting" of the atonement.

And remember, those who do believe in particular atonement aren't denying that Jesus' sacrifice was sufficiently valuable to save everyone: there could be no more valuable sacrifice than the Son of God. The debate is rather over the intention of the cross: who did Jesus come to save? This is important: after all, who would be comfortable with the idea of Jesus failing to complete the task he set out upon? If he was trying to die for everyone, and not everyone ends up saved, then Jesus becomes a semi-successful Savior, thwarted by a greater power. We may begin to wonder what else he will fail in.

Jesus always wins. When he died, he died in union not with the whole world but with his people, and he really saved them. The atonement was particular, and thus powerful and personal. Jesus' love for you, if you're a believer, is therefore powerful and personal too.

3. Unstoppable Love: The Spirit Renews His People

The third and final step in the "moving-from-Adam-to-Christ" process happens when the Holy Spirit unites you to Jesus during your earthly life. God the Father chose you before the world began and gave you to Jesus. Jesus died in union with you nearly 2,000 years ago. Then, on the day you believed the gospel, the Holy Spirit linked you in your own experience to your covenant King.

If you repent and believe, you have all your sins forgiven and receive eternal life. But doesn't this undo all that we've seen so far about salvation being by God alone? Aren't we opening the door again to the idea that, even if God does 95% of the work, I need to do the last 5% by believing in him?

No, salvation is by God alone, by grace alone. Yet how can this be the case if we are the ones who repent and believe? This question finally brings us to the resolution of a tension that runs right through our covenant story. On the one hand, the covenant of grace is conditional at every stage: men and women have to repent and believe. On the other, God seems to make confident assertions that Abraham would certainly have millions of descendants, that heaven would be full. All this seems a muddle until we come to understand Jesus' work in sending his Spirit.

It is the Spirit who brings us from spiritual death to spiritual life. Or, in other words, it is the Spirit who enables us to believe in Jesus, and thus "keep" the covenant of grace.

Paul tells us that "no one seeks for God" (Romans 3:11). Elsewhere he is even starker: "And you were dead in the trespasses and sins in which you once walked" (Ephesians 2:1–2). We are naturally "spiritual zombies," living in the physical sense, but spiritually dead on the inside. Dead people don't choose to believe the gospel. If the gospel was offered to us to accept or reject in our own power, then none of us would ever believe. It would be like putting a life-giving potion next to a coffin and telling the dead person to drink. It doesn't matter how powerful the potion is, a corpse hasn't got the power to reach out and take it.

Thankfully, Jesus sends his Spirit to bring dead people to life. He teaches his disciples, "It is the Spirit who gives life; the flesh is no help at all. The words that I have spoken to you are spirit and life" (John 6:63).

So, how can the covenant of grace be conditional and yet still gracious? Because God himself ensures we fulfill the condition. While believing is something that human beings do (and God does not believe for you), we only do it when he enables us. Faith is therefore a gift of God: "For it has been granted to you that for the sake of Christ you should not only believe in him but also suffer for his sake" (Philippians 1:29). Or summing up the whole salvation process, Paul tells the Ephesians: "For by grace you have been saved through faith. And this is not your own doing; it is the gift of God, not a result of works, so that no one may boast" (Ephesians 2:8–9).

The Holy Spirit loves us too much to let the decision to follow Christ rest in our hands. His love is unstoppable, even by our dead, grimy hearts. When he comes to give us new life, he is simply irresistible. This is the final moment we are united to Jesus: the Holy Spirit comes and makes us "born again," and fills us with the Spirit of the covenant King.

A Gospel of Grace and Hope

If you're a Christian, God has taken 100% ownership of your salvation. All three persons work together to move you from Adam to Christ. Shai Linne summarizes this brilliantly in his aptly titled rap: "Mission Accomplished":

> The Father chooses them,
> the Son gets bruised for them,
> the Spirit renews them.[3]

The gospel is Trinity-shaped, with the three persons working in harmony but distinctly to ensure their plan is successful.

| FATHER CHOOSES | GIVES TO | JESUS DIES FOR | AND FATHER SEND | HOLY SPIRIT BRINGS TO LIFE AND GIVES FAITH |

ETERNITY   AD 33 (ISH)   PRESENT

Those whom the Father chooses, the Son dies for. Those whom the Son dies for, the Spirit renews and gives faith.

Glorious Grace

Earlier, I raised three problems that arise from not holding to this "Reformed" understanding of salvation by God alone. Let's think how the covenantal gospel helps address them.

The Pastoral Problem: Assurance

If any part of my salvation rests on me, I can never be sure I'll make it to heaven. I will spend my life worrying that I might drop the ball at any time. But if salvation is by God alone, I can relax and be humbly confident that I will arrive safely in heaven, because it is God who will get me there. See how Jesus brings all three stages of salvation together to encourage his disciples:

> All that the Father gives me will come to me, and whoever comes to me I will never cast out. For I have come down from heaven, not to do my own will but the will of him who sent me. And this is the will of him who sent me, that I should lose nothing of all that he has given me, but raise it up on the last day.
>
> (John 6:37–39)

Someone may ask, "Can a Christian lose his or her faith?" A more biblical question would be: "Can Jesus lose a sheep?" And as soon as you ask that question, the answer is obvious: of course not.[4] God is not schizophrenic: after choosing us, after sending his Son to die for us, is he then going to let us wander off course during the final leg? Nothing can separate us from the love of God, not even our own spiritual flakiness.

The Theological Problem: The Glory of God

One of the tests Paul uses to discover whether someone has a biblical view of the gospel or not is the principle of boasting. If your gospel allows any room for someone to say, "Well done, me," it is not the Bible's gospel. Now, admittedly almost every theologian or believer would claim that it is wrong for a Christian to boast of their salvation, even if they don't hold to this covenantal gospel. My point, though, is that these brothers and sisters have good hearts *despite*, rather than *because of*, their doctrine.

Our salvation rests on Jesus', not our, willingness to go God's way, and the blessings he earns as covenant King flow to us irresistibly. Is it possible that God might choose someone, Jesus die for them, and then we ruin their plan by refusing to believe, by resisting the Spirit? Of course not! Thankfully, God doesn't respect our "free will" and leave us the power to resist. That way would lead back to the 95%/5% split, and a sharing of the glory for salvation: in other words, there would be room for a little boasting. On the other hand, when God chooses unconditionally, Jesus dies personally and powerfully, and the Holy Spirit gives life irresistibly, we have no option but to join the cry: "To God alone be the glory!"

The Practical Problem

And what about evangelism and prayer? I argued earlier that, if God is not fully and completely sovereign over salvation, there is no point praying: after all, God can do little more than try and arrange circumstances so as to make it as easy as possible for someone to come to faith. What he cannot do is ensure it happens. Hopefully, we have seen by now that this is not the case. But does the idea of a totally sovereign God make prayer and evangelism pointless? After all, if he already knows who's going to be saved, why pray?

The simplest answer is: because God tells us to. Mysteriously (and there's no getting around that mystery), God uses our prayers and evangelism as the means by which he brings people to faith. It is a privilege to be given the role of God's coworker. Despite being crystal clear that God is completely in control of his universe and sovereign over salvation, the apostle Paul can still encourage the Romans to get busy with evangelism:

> How then will they call on him in whom they have not believed? And how are they to believe in him of whom they have never heard? And how are they to hear without someone preaching? And how are they to preach unless they are sent? As it is written, "How beautiful are the feet of those who preach the good news!" (Romans 10:14–15)

The Bible unashamedly holds together God's sovereignty and our responsibility. Our problem is that we can't understand how both are true. We get ourselves stuck in the "Pinocchio problem."

At the beginning of the film, Pinocchio is a wooden puppet, with Geppetto, his creator, quite literally pulling the strings. Geppetto has total control; Pinocchio has no heart or mind of his own. With a swish of the fairy's wand though, Pinocchio becomes a real boy, able to think, move, and make decisions for himself. Suddenly, Geppetto has no control whatsoever over his creation.

We think that these are the only two options: either the Creator has control and we creatures are mere puppets, or we human beings are "real boys" and God is as helpless as Geppetto when it comes to controlling our hearts. In fact, the

Bible describes a third situation. We are thinking, responsible people: real boys and girls. At the same time, God is fully sovereign: Geppetto on a cosmic scale. How can both be true? I don't know. Neither does anyone else. What we're called to do is trust that God is a sufficiently wise and intelligent Creator to make a universe where we are responsible and not robots, and yet he remains totally in control of our every decision.

This gives us confidence in prayer: God is both willing and able to change a person's heart from unbelief to faith. It also gives us great confidence in evangelism: in the big picture, it will succeed. God will not be thwarted by human sinfulness. Our job is to explain the message of Jesus, not engineer results. We do not need to pressurize or manipulate: it is the Holy Spirit who gives life, and he's able to convert even the hardest sinner.

Nor should we have any worries about proclaiming Jesus as the Savior of the world. Sometimes, those who've come to believe all the Bible has to say about predestination and particular atonement begin to panic that calling Jesus the Savior of the world is misleading. Should we instead only talk about Jesus being the Savior of the *church*? The Puritan minister Thomas Boston makes the comparison between Jesus and a doctor (or physician): "One having a commission to be the physician of a society, is the physician of the whole society, by office; and so stands related to every man of them, as his physician: howbeit, he is not actually a healer to any of them, but such as employ him." The village doctor is still worthy of the title "village doctor" whether all the villagers use him or not. Jesus is the Savior of the world, and can be announced as such to the whole world, without fussing over whether everyone listening will accept him. As Christians, we are to be promiscuous with the gospel, spreading it wherever we can, leaving the results to God.

Rediscovering this gospel of grace alone is incredibly freeing and empowering. Suddenly, my weaknesses, sins, and inadequacies are no impediment to God keeping and using me in the service of his kingdom. Grace starts, sustains, and sees us home safely.

10

COVENANT PEOPLE

ONE OF THE CONSEQUENCES of God uniting us to Jesus is that we become united to the rest of his people too. Jesus does not save people one by one, only to put them into individually sealed packages, like a row of Barbie and Ken dolls on a toyshop shelf. Instead, he binds them as closely to one another as he does to himself. Now, we'll focus on the people that the covenant creates.

Jesus' One Body

In the village where I used to live there were five churches: Methodist, Baptist, Roman Catholic, Church of England, and Independent Charismatic. In the city where I now live, I couldn't even begin to count. Sometimes, there are good and necessary reasons for all these denominations, but they are only a temporary state of affairs. From God's point of view, there is only one church. Speaking of the former difference between Jews and Gentiles, Paul says,

> But now in Christ Jesus you who once were far off have been
> brought near by the blood of Christ. For he himself is our peace,
> who has made us both one and has broken down in his flesh the
> dividing wall of hostility by abolishing the law of commandments
> expressed in ordinances, that he might create in himself one new
> man in place of the two, so making peace, and might reconcile
> us both to God in one body through the cross, thereby killing
> the hostility.
> (Ephesians 2:13–16)

Christians are "one new man" and "one body." As soon as you
become a Christian, you become a member of Jesus' body: in
other words, the church. Elsewhere Jesus is described as the
head of the church, and a head can only be head of one body.
In this sense, there is only ever one church, one people of God.
From what we have seen of the covenant, this makes sense.
You can either be in Adam or in Christ: there is no third option.

Paul also says that Jews and Greeks are one in Christ. This
is tremendously important: there is not one set of promises
for Jews in the Old Testament and a completely different
set for everyone else in the New. No, all the way through, the
deal has been the same: if you trust in God's covenant gospel,
he will forgive your sins and welcome you into his kingdom.
Of course, in the Old Testament the majority of God's people
were also ethnically Jewish. This is one of the significant
changes in the new covenant: the gospel goes international
and forms a people of every tribe, nation, and tongue. And
these newcomers to the covenant people don't form a separate
group, but are united to the faithful children of Abraham who
have been believing for millennia. In Romans 11, Paul compares
Gentile (non-Jewish) Christians to branches grafted into an
olive tree. There is only one tree, but it's possible to add in new

branches. So it is with Jesus' people: he has one "covenant community" which began when Adam first believed the promise about the serpent-crusher. Since then, Jesus has been building this body, and will continue to do so until he returns for the final time. One covenant means one community. This is what the Nicene Creed is talking about when it speaks of "One, Holy, Catholic, Apostolic Church." Ultimately, there is only one church, built on the gospel preached by the apostles, and "catholic," not in the sense of Roman Catholic, but small "c" catholic, meaning universal.

Jesus' Many Bodies

Interestingly, Paul is happy to apply the picture of the church being Christ's body not just to all Christians everywhere, but also to specific congregations. He encourages the church in Corinth to give themselves in service to one another, as they are one body (1 Corinthians 12). It's relatively comfortable to accept that you're united in Christ to Paul, Luther, or even a Christian thousands of miles away in another country. The great thing about Luther is that he's rather unlikely to want help decorating his lounge, or to pop round for a chat when you're dying to have a quiet night in. It's the forty people we sit with on a Sunday who are our prime focus, says Paul. Don't kid yourself that you love the church, or even that you love Jesus, if you're not prepared to love the particular people he has put you in fellowship with.

All of which means that church really matters. It's not simply another club we join. Indeed, our fellow church members are our body. Like it or not, you are as closely connected to the specific people in your congregation as you are to Jesus. And sticking with the body imagery, you are as tightly bound to them as your hand is to your arm.

It might be worth pausing right now to ask yourself whether your life reflects this? Many of us are happy to become relatively close to a handful of "people like us." But to others, the less socially able, the less intelligent, the less wealthy, we effectively say, "Get lost." Yet, these are the people Jesus was happy to unite to himself. Are we honestly going to look at a part of Jesus' body and say, "Not good enough for me." Imagine Jesus walking into the room. Would you dare look at him and say, "Jesus, great to meet you at last! But I don't like your ears. And for that matter, that nose is pretty hideous." That is effectively what we're doing when we subtly "cut off" people in our congregations who we don't instantly take to. If Jesus welcomes them, then so should we. After all, we have no more right to be in covenant than they do.

Church Government: Circles, Chains, and Pyramids
So the word "church" can mean either all Christians everywhere or one specific congregation. Paul begins his letter with: "To the church of God that is in Corinth," not: "To the little bit of the church that is in Corinth." He can call Corinth a body—rather than an arm, with the Ephesians being the leg, the Romans the neck, the Galatians one eye, the Colossians the other, and so on. When it comes to organizing congregations, somehow we have to find a way of doing justice to both these ways of speaking of church.

There have been three major approaches.

Independent: Circles
First is the Independent model. While these guys would recognize that ultimately we're all one in Christ, they don't think that unity should be reflected structurally in the visible church. Each congregation is its own separate unit. Each has

its own leadership, who—while, if they're wise, will keep in regular contact with other church leaders—bear no responsibility for them or their congregations. Power resides ultimately in the congregation, and it is to them alone that the leadership is accountable. That's why we could picture each independent church as its own separate circle (see diagram below).

Presbyterian: Chain-Links

The other two models attempt to demonstrate the unity of the church in their organizational structures. Like Independents, Presbyterians appoint elders over each congregation and see each as its own church, but they are also happy to talk about being in the same church as other congregations in their denomination. The elders of the different congregations are accountable both to their own flocks and to the other elders. Typically, all the elders will meet up a handful of times a year for accountability and encouragement. I'd picture Presbyterianism like a chain: each congregation is interlinked, but also remains its own distinct unit.

Episcopalian: Pyramid

Finally, Episcopalians (Roman Catholics, the Orthodox churches, Anglicans) also see their whole denomination as one church. You might be a member of St. Stephen's in Barnstaple, but you are in the same church as the Vicar of St. Teresa's, Barnsley, or for that matter the Archbishop of Canterbury. They differ from Presbyterians and Independents on the question of who leads the church. Whereas Independents and Presbyterians typically have just two church offices (elder and deacon), Episcopalians have (at least) three. The bishop is a rank above the ministers of churches, and has spiritual responsibility and oversight for them. Some churches, such as the

Church of England, combine Episcopacy with a form of what is known as Erastianism: the idea that the national government or sovereign is the earthly governor of the church. We could picture this more hierarchical set-up like a pyramid: all churches being part of the greater structure, but with a more elaborate set of officials "above" the normal Christian.

To my mind, the Presbyterian system seems the most natural outworking of the Bible's teaching. Certainly, Paul saw bishops, elders, teachers, and pastors as the same role: he uses the terms interchangeably to refer to the same people in Acts 20 and Titus 1. This would seem to rule out Episcopacy. It also seems that at times the whole church could meet together to make decisions that affect more than just the local congregation (Acts 15), and this, together with the fact that it would seem natural to want to reflect the oneness of the church in its actual earthly structures (John 17:20–24), suggests Presbyterian rather than Independent church government.

While these are matters on which Bible-loving Christians disagree, they cannot simply be waved away as "secondary issues." God has spoken about the structure of church government in his Word: presumably, he wants us to listen. The church is the guardian of the gospel, particularly through its leaders.

Or, we might even say that the Bible is not enough to ensure the health of the church and evangelization of the world. If the Bible was all we needed, God could have sent Gabriel and the angels to airdrop ready-translated Scriptures into every household. Instead, he entrusted the protection and preaching of the gospel to the church, and in particular to its leaders. He clearly expects us to play a part, as we'd expect from all we've seen about covenants. Churches, therefore, need *both* the Bible and healthy leadership in order to be faithful.

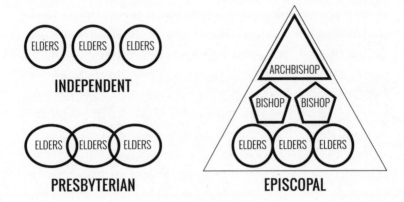

A church that has nice leaders with no doctrine is a disaster. A church that has a sound doctrinal basis, but allows its ministers to get away with murder (almost), is no better.

Covenant Signs

But how can you tell who are members of this one great covenant community? Or, for that matter, members of your local church? At each stage of the covenant of grace, God gives a physical sign to identify those who belong to his people. For example, God said to Abraham,

> As for you, you shall keep my covenant, you and your offspring after you throughout their generations. This is my covenant, which you shall keep, between me and you and your offspring after you: Every male among you shall be circumcised. You shall be circumcised in the flesh of your foreskins, and it shall be a sign of the covenant between me and you. He who is eight days old among you shall be circumcised . . . Any uncircumcised male who is not circumcised in the flesh of his foreskin shall be cut off from his people; he has broken my covenant.
>
> (Genesis 17:9–12, 14)

If we were to look at these verses alone, we might conclude that the condition of God's covenant with Abraham was simply circumcision. If you get circumcised, you're keeping it; if you don't, you're breaking it. Yet, earlier we saw that faith was the condition of the covenant of grace (Genesis 15:6; Romans 4:11). Has God contradicted himself? Not at all: "[Abraham] received the sign of circumcision as a seal of the righteousness that he had by faith while he was still uncircumcised" (Romans 4:11). Circumcision was not a sign simply of being Jewish, physically descended from Abraham. It was meant to be a sign of having *faith* and therefore being justified, a physical sign of a spiritual reality.

In a sense, therefore, anyone who had been circumcised was a member of the covenant. Yet, those who had the sign without the reality of the faith to which it was meant to point were not truly members of God's people: without faith, no one is united to Christ and no one will inherit his blessings.

Visible/Invisible

Here, theologians have helpfully made a distinction between the visible church and the invisible church. The invisible church is the group of true believers, made up of all those whom God the Father chose, God the Son died for, and God the Spirit renewed. So, Abraham is a member of the invisible church, as is Moses, Mary, Peter, Timothy, Augustine, John Wesley, and Billy Graham. The reason why theologians have called it the "invisible church" is that it is impossible for human beings to know for certain who is in this group. You or I can't see for sure whether someone is born again; only God can. (So, to God, the invisible church is in fact visible!)

The visible church, on the other hand, is the church that is visible to human beings, made up of all those who profess to follow Christ and therefore take on the covenant sign, together with their children. This group includes all those in the invisible church, but also everyone who for a while seems to be a Christian, but then turns back. Take Judas, for example. He was a circumcised descendant of Abraham. In that sense, he was a member of the outward covenant community, the visible church. Scripture seems pretty clear, however, that he was never truly "born again": so he was not a member of the invisible church, not truly "in Christ."

This is what Paul has in mind when he says, "For not all who are descended from Israel belong to Israel, and not all are children of Abraham because they are his offspring" (Romans 9:6–7).

Anyone who was physically descended from Israel, another name for Jacob, was in one sense a member of the people of God. But, of course, many, many of them didn't believe. So, in another sense, they were not truly part of the covenant community.

The New Covenant
This distinction between outward and inward membership of the covenant continues into the new covenant. The New Testament gives us plenty of examples of people who seemed to have accepted the gospel, and were therefore welcomed into the church, but who later revealed themselves never to have sincerely believed. In other words, it's possible in this sense to be in covenant with God, but without believing: "But false prophets also arose among the people, just as there will be false teachers among you, who will secretly bring in destructive heresies, even denying the Master who bought them, bringing upon themselves swift destruction" (2 Peter 2:1). Who is Peter talking about? We might initially be tempted to say simply,

"non-Christians." After all, they are teachers of heresy that leads other people (as well as themselves) to be destroyed by Jesus. But tucked away in the middle of the verse is that little phrase: "denying the Master who bought them." In some sense, Jesus owns these people in a different way from the way in which he owns every human being. Normally, the language of "buying" is linked to salvation, but we've seen already that Jesus never loses those who are genuinely saved. We therefore need a third category, between "pagan" and "real Christian," to account for these people.

The most obvious, given all we've seen throughout the Old Testament, is "covenant-breaker." The book of Hebrews talks about people who have been "enlightened," "tasted the heavenly gift," and even "shared in the Holy Spirit" subsequently falling away (Hebrews 6). How can God describe people in such exalted terms, and yet they still fall away? Unless we undo all we've seen so far about born-again Christians never losing their salvation (and therefore let the Bible contradict itself), we *must* find another explanation. The simplest by far is that these people were, like Judas, outward members of the covenant community, but then threw in the towel. In this sense, they are "covenant-breakers." They have been baptized, participated in church life, but never truly believed.

This means we can divide humanity into three categories: non-Christians, covenant-breakers, and covenant-keepers. Of these, only covenant-keepers are truly saved. The sorts of passages we have looked at warn those of us who profess to be part of the covenant community never to abandon our faith: to whom much has been given, much will be expected. It is a terrible thing to commit to, and then turn your back on, the Lord of whom you know so much.

Baptism: Who's In?

Let's return to the question: how are we meant to know who is in the covenant community if we can't see people's faith? How can we tell who is in the church? Well, given there's only one covenant of grace, everything works more or less the same as it always has. We are called to have faith and receive the sign of the covenant. That sign, though, is no longer circumcision but baptism. Baptism does not magically give new life, but is a sign that (among other things) we are members of the new covenant. It does the same job as circumcision did in the Abrahamic edition of the covenant (Romans 4:11; Colossians 2:11–12).

Once we realize that we are in the same covenant as Abraham, albeit an updated edition, we are also in a position to answer one of the most debated questions among evangelicals: who should get baptized? Everyone agrees that non-Christians who convert should. But what about their children?

Think back to circumcision. It was a sign of Abraham's *faith*, and hence justification (Romans 4:11). And yet, God tells him to circumcise his sons when they are eight days old (Genesis 17:12). There is no doubt or debate: children of believers during the Abrahamic, Mosaic, and Davidic eras were in covenant with God and were thus entitled to the covenant sign. They were to be treated as inside, rather than outside, God's family. They were entitled to take part in the worship of Israel, participating in the festivals and sacrifices. They were subject to the laws of Israel.

Non-covenant members were barred from all these privileges. The children of Pharaoh could not worship at the temple, pray to God, or join in the family festivals. Neither were they expected to keep the specific covenant laws. They were outsiders.

But Israelite children were in. This doesn't mean that every child born to an Israelite was certainly saved. Many were not "internally" in covenant. But they were granted the right as children to belong to the family of God, because their parents were members.

Baptism and circumcision are both signs of faith. It therefore makes sense that children of Christians should receive the covenant sign, just as the children of Old Testament covenant members did. We are, after all, in essentially the same covenant as them, albeit an updated edition. The Puritans used different pictures to try to illustrate this unity. One compared the covenant of grace to a flower growing and blossoming. The full bloom is of course more glorious than the seed or the shoot, but is not a different entity. Another compared the covenant of grace to the sun rising. Slowly, more and more light is shed on the earth, but the sun itself remains the same.

The basic question is: "Are children of believers inside or outside the covenant of grace?" Or, are they to be counted as insiders or outsiders at church? In the Old Testament, they were in. Is it really the case that, with the more glorious final edition of the covenant, they have all been ejected?

Imagine a Jew, let's call him Reuben, listening to Peter preach on the day of Pentecost. Reuben is standing cradling his newborn twins Daniel and David in his arms. Reuben rightly understands that as things stand, the boys are currently members of God's covenant people. He doesn't know whether they believe or not: after all they're only six weeks old. But Daniel and David are certainly "insiders," not in the same place as the pagan Roman soldier standing looking on.

So, Peter preaches away, and announces the dawn of the new covenant. "Great," thinks Reuben, "just what we've been waiting for!" With the other 3,000, Reuben gets baptized at the end of Peter's sermon, realizing that baptism is now the replacement of the circumcision he underwent as a baby. But what of Daniel and David? Reuben has listened carefully to Peter: "For the promise is for you and for your children and for all who are far off, everyone whom the Lord our God calls to himself" (Acts 2:39). Trained in several thousand years of God's covenant story, Reuben would surely have understood this to mean that his twins were still members of the covenant family. Just as before, there was no guarantee the children were "born again." But just as before, that wasn't the point: the signs were signs of being part of the covenant community.

The position I am arguing for here is called "paedobaptism" (*paedos* being the Greek word for child). Of course, there are many Bible-believing evangelicals who would disagree. So, here are a few quick bullet points to clarify and supplement the argument. Think of these as headlines to explore further, rather than fully fleshed-out arguments in and of themselves.

- If children were no longer "in" the family, why is this never mentioned? Why is there no debate in the New Testament, largely Jewish church as there is over circumcision, food laws, and other Old Testament practices? It seems unlikely that the ejection of children would be the one thing that was easily accepted.
- In 1 Corinthians 7:14, Paul describes as "holy" the children of a marriage where one parent is Christian and the other not, on the grounds that *one* parent believes. What does it mean for a child to be "holy" because mother believes? It can't mean "born again," as a mother's faith doesn't guarantee a child's. It refers instead to being set apart for God, separate from the world: in other words in covenant, *externally* at least.

- When parents bring their children to Jesus, he welcomes and blesses them, and teaches that the kingdom belongs to "such as these." While "such as these" includes *more* than those particular children, it cannot exclude those literally in front of Jesus.
- Acts and 1 Corinthians talk about whole households being baptized. These, most likely, contained children, baptized because of the head of the household's faith.
- Children are addressed as part of the church in Paul's letters (Ephesians 6:1) and expected to obey "in the Lord."
- The vast majority of Reformed theologians and other church "greats" have been paedobaptists. A sample list would include: Luther, Calvin, John Owen, Thomas Cranmer, Jonathan Edwards, Francis Turretin, John Wesley, George Whitefield, J. C. Ryle, B. B. Warfield, John Stott, and J. I. Packer. It was comfortably the majority position among the Puritans.
- Are our children really in the same position before God as those of a non-Christian neighbor? If so, they should not be allowed the privileges of covenant membership: for example, prayer. "Our Father" is not a prayer for non-Christians.

Typically, this position prompts the question: "What about those children who grow up and abandon the faith?" They are covenant-breakers. After all, baptism is not a guarantee of faith. Those who are born into the covenant externally can still break it unless they turn to Christ themselves. Occasionally, people object to this by pointing out that, according to the prophecies of Jeremiah and Ezekiel, the new covenant will be written on the heart, and contain only those who have the Holy Spirit. But, as we've seen already, the new covenant contains both "now" and "not-yet" elements. Those same prophecies predicted a renewed earth, for example. Given that the New Testament is happy to talk about people who are "bought" by Jesus but then end up in hell, it seems that the category of covenant breaker still remains for us living in the "now."[1] The "unbreakableness" of the new covenant will only fully be seen after Jesus returns.

Discipline and Dinner

So, those who profess faith and are baptized, together with their children, are to be treated as members of the covenant of grace, members of the church. God alone knows whose names are written in the book of life, so until the last day this is the best we can do. But why do we even need to know? Can't we just leave it to God? Why do *we* need a method of determining who else is in God's family?

One reason is that we are told to care for one another. Most of the time, this will involve informal conversations, with a mixture of encouragement, teaching, correction, and rebuke. But occasionally, a church member wanders further from the flock and gets into serious trouble. If a professing Christian commits serious sin and refuses to repent, then it is up to the church, led by the elders, to discipline them. There are plenty of examples of this in the Bible, yet, as a practice, "church discipline" is worryingly rare. One of the most startling passages is 1 Corinthians 5:

> I wrote to you in my letter not to associate with sexually immoral people—not at all meaning the sexually immoral of this world, or the greedy and swindlers, or idolaters, since then you would need to go out of the world. But now I am writing to you not to associate with anyone who bears the name of brother if he is

guilty of sexual immorality or greed, or is an idolater, reviler, drunkard, or swindler—not even to eat with such a one. For what have I to do with judging outsiders? Is it not those inside the church whom you are to judge? God judges those outside. "Purge the evil person from among you."

(1 Corinthians 5:9–13)

Paul is dealing with a church that has no problems with one of its members sleeping with his mother-in-law. It seems they have misunderstood the nature of grace. Grace is not a license to sin: real grace, as we saw earlier, produces the fruit of holy lives, however imperfectly. How should churches react to someone who is "sinning big" but refusing to repent? They should judge them and throw them out!

This is not just rank judgmentalism. Discipline aims to restore the guilty party: the shock of losing fellowship is an attempt to restore them to their senses. Discipline is loving. It is also motivated by a love for Christ. If the church is his visible body, it matters how we behave: the world is watching.

The Lord's Supper

Christians disagree as to how exactly this discipline is to be worked out in practice, but notice that the Corinthians are told not to eat with the person. This may mean meals in general, but quite likely refers to the Lord's Supper or communion.

Alongside baptism, communion is the second sacrament or sign given to the church. Whereas baptism is the entry sign, communion is the sign of continuing in Christ.

For a long time, I have to confess I went to communion services rather reluctantly. To my mind, they were simply normal services with a ritual tagged on the end that delayed coffee. I knew it was good to be reminded of Jesus' death for me, but it all seemed a bit random: the preacher had likely just reminded me of that anyway.

But there is more to the Lord's Supper than just remembering, important though remembering is. Paul calls it a "participation" in the blood and body of Christ. While the bread and wine are not magically transformed into Christ's body and blood, and do not automatically give us any blessing, neither are they only reminders to our brains. When received with faith, they are strengtheners of our communion with Christ, another means of grace through which God protects and grows his children. This purpose of communion is beautifully summed up in the answer to question 77 of the Heidelberg Catechism, a set of questions and answers written back in the sixteenth century to help believers understand their faith. Communion, we are told, enables us "to become more and more united to his sacred body, by the Holy Ghost, who dwells both in Christ and in us; so that we, though Christ is in heaven and we on earth, are notwithstanding 'flesh of his flesh and bone of his bone.'"

The unrepentant sinner is to be excluded from this meal. While you cannot "unbaptize" someone, you can prevent them from sharing in the Lord's Supper, the meal that says, "We are one family in Christ and are trusting in his death to atone for our sin." By taking communion, you are recognizing that sin deserves death; that is what the broken bread and wine symbolize. To do this while refusing to repent, or while refusing to participate in the fellowship God has put you in, is hypocrisy.

But notice that Paul says we are not to judge the world. Those outside the covenant cannot be subject to church discipline, for the simple reason that they are not in the church! Hence the need to be clear, to the best of our ability, who's in and who's out, who therefore we are particularly responsible for shepherding and disciplining.

For those who know their sins are scarlet, but God's gospel washes them as clean as snow, communion is a joyous reminder of their place at Jesus' banquet to come, a fantastic family celebration, a proclamation of the saving death of their Lord, and spiritual food for the journey ahead.

And it is to that journey we now turn, to discover just what life under the covenant should look like for faithful pilgrims.

11

COVENANT LIFE

A YEAR OR TWO AGO, I conducted a highly unscientific
survey before church one Sunday. The question was simple:
"Why did Jesus come?" Most people gave answers that
revolved around the themes: "To die for us," "To forgive us,"
and "To rescue us from sin." All good stuff. When I pushed
further, Jesus' teaching, resurrection, and life as an example
all came up. Interestingly, no one gave the answer that John
the Baptist provides: "And [John] preached, saying, 'After me
comes he who is mightier than I, the strap of whose sandals
I am not worthy to stoop down and untie. I have baptized
you with water, but he will baptize you with the Holy Spirit'"
(Mark 1:7–8).

Jesus is coming to baptize his people with the Holy Spirit.
For some people, this is almost *all* Jesus is about: they aren't
much interested in the cross and only care about the Spirit.
Clearly, this is an unbalanced view. But for others, this role of
Jesus is all but ignored. Is baptizing with the Spirit a central
part of your understanding of Jesus' work, or just something

swept aside as an awkward detail, a matter of, at best, secondary importance? If so, you're out of line with the man described by Jesus as the greatest of the prophets.

If baptizing with the Spirit is one of the main reasons why Jesus came, we can quickly set aside the idea that "Spirit baptism" is just something for the elite, the higher grade Christians who have undergone some extra experience separate from their initial conversion. Paul makes it clear that, if you're a Christian, you've been baptized with the Spirit: "For in one Spirit we were all baptized into one body—Jews or Greeks, slaves or free—and all were made to drink of one Spirit" (1 Corinthians 12:13). There's only one body of Christ, the church. And there's only one way into that body: Spirit baptism. Therefore, whoever you are, if you're Christian and a true member of the church, you've been baptized with the Spirit.

But this doesn't really help us understand *what* Spirit baptism is. To do this, let's back up and follow the story of Jesus and the Spirit.

Inseparable Companions
Luke traces this theme through his Gospel. He starts by telling us that Jesus was conceived by the power of the Holy Spirit (Luke 1:35). Jesus had no human father, so it was the Holy Spirit who brought Jesus to life in Mary's womb. Right from his birth, Jesus was Spirit-filled.

When he turned thirty, Jesus began his ministry by being baptized by John. On this occasion, the Holy Spirit came down on him again: although he already had the Spirit, he was further "filled" as he began his public work (Luke 3:21–22). Jesus' first job is to overcome Satan's temptation, and we are told it is the Spirit who leads Jesus into conflict with the devil (Luke 4:1–2). Jesus is tempted by the most skilled tempter, in the harshest conditions, and yet he resists. The Spirit enables him to beat Satan.

It is the Spirit who then accompanies him on his preaching mission (Luke 4:16–21). The Spirit has anointed Jesus to be the preacher of the gospel. Everywhere that Jesus goes, the Spirit goes: they are constant companions. Jesus is the perfect Spirit-filled man, always relying on the Spirit for power. Of course, Jesus is God too, but we shouldn't use this to undermine the fact that he was fully human, like us. Like us, he needed to pray, rely on God, and even grow in his understanding (Luke 2:52). In fact, if he hadn't done all this as man, he would never have fulfilled the covenant of works for us—after all, the covenant is between God and human beings, not God and God.

The Spirit therefore accompanies Jesus right to death. Hebrews 9:14 tells us that he offered himself as a sacrifice on the cross "through the eternal Spirit": it was the Spirit who sustained him, even through the torment of the cross, before providing the power to raise him from the dead (1 Peter 3:18).

In his first sermon in the book of Acts, Peter tells us that after his ascension Jesus yet again receives the Spirit from his Father. Now, Jesus has the Spirit not just for himself, but in order to pour it out on his people (Acts 2:33), to bring about the Spirit baptism that John promised. But still the question remains—why? What does this Spirit-baptism do?

The Power to Obey
A clue to one of the primary purposes comes in the events surrounding the day the Spirit is poured out, the day of Pentecost. As Luke describes the scene in the first two chapters of Acts, we read of a great leader, Jesus, going up in a cloud, fire and rushing thunder coming down, and his people gathered

below being filled with the Spirit. Luke is reminding us of another great covenant-making day, the day Moses went up into the cloud above Mount Sinai, fire and rushing winds thundered, and down came the Ten Commandments. That day, the people learned they needed to be holy—but failed badly. This time, instead of just bringing down rules, one far greater than Moses sends his Spirit down. To highlight the difference, 3,000 people believe, the exact same number we are told rebelled and were killed in the incident of the golden calf at Sinai.[1]

The Spirit, in other words, is bringing life and holiness. He is, after all, the *Holy* Spirit. What we are seeing fulfilled is God's new covenant promise that he would put his Spirit in his people to make sure they obeyed and lived faithful lives. The Spirit alone brings the power to obey.

How does he do this? He connects us to Jesus, the perfect Spirit-filled man. We've seen several times already that salvation is all about union with Christ. So far, we have concentrated on what you might call the legal aspects of that union: Jesus standing in our place under the curse and giving us his perfect record. But being united to Jesus also has experiential, life-giving benefits too. Perhaps the most famous picture of this is in John 15, where Jesus refers to himself as a vine with his people as branches. We are organically united, we might say. It is the Holy Spirit who connects us like this to Jesus. He is the lifeline between Jesus in heaven and us on earth; through the Holy Spirit, all the power of Jesus as man can flow to us.

This is why the Holy Spirit is sometimes called the Spirit of Jesus. In fact, in Romans 8, Paul switches between talking about the Holy Spirit being in us and Jesus himself being in us. How can Jesus be living in us, if he's in heaven? Through the filling of the Holy Spirit.

We now begin to see the importance of the Spirit being with Jesus all through his life on earth. The Spirit you have in you today is the same Spirit who resisted the temptations of Satan in the desert. He is the Spirit who enabled Jesus to preach the gospel fearlessly, the Spirit who sustained Jesus through all his suffering, even on the cross, the Spirit who gave Jesus resurrection life. Jesus managed all this not by switching off his humanity and doing it all as God. Rather, as man, he conquered through the power of the Spirit.

So, when we read passages that call us to live holy lives, we need to remember that we are as closely connected to Jesus as a branch is to a vine, our hand is to our arm: we are one body, one organism with him. Alone, we don't have the power to resist Satan or sin, but he's already done it. And he did it as a human being, not just as God. We therefore have access to "human holiness," everything we need to fight the battle ourselves. We don't have to create our own holiness from scratch; we need to trust Jesus and drink in the ability to live a holy life from him, through the Spirit.

None of this is meant to suggest that holiness is easy. Sanctification is not the same as justification, where *all* the work is done by God and God alone. On the contrary, Paul talks about struggling and straining to grow in godliness.

But unless Jesus had "grown" this human holiness first, all our struggles would be in vain. Now, full of his Spirit and connected like branches to the tree of life, we can make progress. It's something like the apps you download to your smartphone. Your success in, say, finding your way around a city is dependent *both* on the manufacturer making a map available *and* you opening it up, and using it to get walking. The whole point of downloading an app is to use it—just having a map or a language translator in the app store is no use unless you open it up and start typing. But, equally, you'd never take a step in the right direction if the app had not been created for you by someone else.

So Jesus is seated in heaven, with all the holiness you need. He has the "sexual purity" app and the "prayerfulness" app. He has the "zeal for evangelism" app and the "patience" app. On and on we could go. And everything is available for download.

If we try to go it alone, without coming to the One who has all the resources we require, we'll fall flat. If we forget that the resources are there at all, we'll give up. But if we prayerfully come to him, ask for the holiness gifts we need in battle day to day, and then try our best humbly to put them to work, Jesus promises that we will make progress.

The Path to Obey

What will that progress look like? In a sense, we've answered that question already. God initially wanted a world full of little images, and nothing has changed. Each covenant since the garden has called for God's people to obey his law, which will reshape us back into his image. God's law lays out the path which the Spirit empowers us to walk.

Although there's some disagreement among Christians here, most of those who recognize the significance of the Bible's covenants point to the Ten Commandments as a good summary of the rules that help us live God-reflecting lives. No matter whether you are Noah on his ark, Moses in the desert, Paul on a missionary journey, or Jane Bloggs in twenty-first-century England, you have to obey the Ten Commandments.

Have to? Doesn't that sound a bit legalistic? I thought we were under grace, not law? And so we are—Paul says as much. But when we read the word "law" in the Bible, it can mean all sorts of different things. Sometimes, it means "obeying rules to get right with God." In that sense, Christians are certainly not under law.[2] At other times, it refers to the Mosaic edition of the covenant—and again we are no longer under law in this way. To hold on to this earlier edition of the covenant of grace would be like holding on to a winning lottery ticket and refusing to cash it in for the money it promised—a good document becomes useless.[3] Or, if we think that it is by getting circumcised, not eating pork, and wearing tasseled robes that we get right with God, we have turned a covenant that was meant to be gracious into a legalistic means of self-justification. This problem seems to have arisen in the early church, and explains why Paul can at times sound very condemning of the Mosaic covenant. In and of itself, it was gracious, but when misused—either by concentrating on the rules without the rescue, or by rejecting Jesus, the reality to which all the ceremonies pointed—Moses becomes a covenant of works, condemning and killing.[4]

This, incidentally, is why we don't obey all the rules set out during that era of the covenant story. Occasionally, Christians who claim to follow the Bible are mocked and asked why they don't therefore avoid eating shellfish, as Leviticus commands.

I once attended a meeting of church leaders where another minister objected to me appealing to the Bible on a particular matter. He started pulling my shirt and telling me that, if I really trusted the Bible so much, I wouldn't wear clothes of mixed materials, as this is clearly prohibited in Leviticus 19:19.

With respect, this is incredibly infantile. From the earliest days of the church, Christians realized that the new covenant brought about a different way of relating to the laws laid out by Moses. Several of those laws concerned ceremonies that pointed forward to Jesus' sacrifice—rules about circumcision, festivals, and the temple, for example. These ceremonial laws are no longer to be followed *directly*, but rather to be obeyed by trusting in the reality to which the ceremony pointed: Jesus himself. Also included in this category are those laws concerning clothing and food, a pointer to the day when God's international people would stand out because of their holiness. Jesus himself says that these laws no longer bind us.[5]

Then there are laws that we might call "civil" laws. As Israel was a nation state, it needed national laws, as modern countries do today. We have speed limits, for example, and rules about which side of the road to drive on, but they vary from country to country: living in England, the French speed limit is not my direct concern. Now that God's people are no longer confined to one country (Israel), these laws have been abolished, though we can learn from what the Westminster Confession calls their "general equity." The idea here is that, while we don't apply the law directly, we can learn from its underlying principle. For example, the Israelites were told that, if they found themselves in a neighbor's vineyard, they could pick some grapes, but not walk away with a basketful.[6] As England is not a particularly vine-rich country, the general equity of the law might help me realize that, while grabbing a coke from my friend's fridge is probably OK, going around with a backpack and emptying his drinks cabinet is probably less so.

But alongside these ceremonial and civil laws are moral laws. These were the same before and after the period of the Mosaic covenant, and are summarized in the Ten Commandments. We never see God caring whether or not non-Israelites eat prawns or wear clothes made of many materials. Nor does he care about these things before or after the covenant era of Moses. Ceremonial and civil laws are bracketed by geography (just Israel) and history (just Moses to Jesus). On the other hand, we always see God caring about murder, adultery, and idolatry, wherever and whenever you find yourself in human history. So the Ten Commandments provide a summary of the law all humankind is called to obey.[7] It's just never OK to murder, lie, or dishonor your parents.

Jesus himself seems well able to distinguish between which laws are temporary and which are eternal: the Ten Commandments form the basis of his Sermon on the Mount, where he shows the depth and heart-driven obedience the commandments were always meant to imply.

Law and Gospel

So, the law (as straight commands) cannot save us, but it does show us the kind of people God wants us to be. It convicts us of our sin, and then, after we've applied the gospel, teaches us how to live. If you think about it, these two functions must go together. When I read: "Do not gossip" and am convicted, I should move to the gospel, repenting of my sin and rejoicing in God's forgiveness. But what to do when I get up from my knees to carry on with life? Well, God still doesn't want me to gossip, so I should take that command and obey it. Law and gospel are not enemies, but friends, when understood rightly.

Law without gospel is powerless; gospel without law is point-less. Christ came to save us *from* sin, not *for* sin.

Now, grace and works *are* enemies. But sanctification and justification are not; both are blessings of union with Christ. Think back to Noah. What saved him? God's gracious "gospel," of course. But what path did that grace send Noah down in order to reach the end goal of salvation? He had to obey God's commands—very specifically, to build an ark. Would he have been saved if he had ignored the command and just sat back reveling in the fact that God loved him and had chosen him? No, he'd have drowned. In that sense, "law" and gospel worked together to save Noah—but as one who was in union with Christ, he was saved by grace alone, through faith alone. This grace moved Noah to believe, and then to obey.

Similarly, with us. We are commanded to repent and believe—itself a sort of "law," we might even say. Is that legalistic? No, it's no different from saying the covenant of grace (or the gospel) has conditions. The gospel contains "law" in this very narrow sense. And yet, it remains a gospel of salvation by grace alone. Why? Because, as we saw in the covenant of redemption, Christ alone supplies the power to repent and believe.

Equally, time after time, we are told to obey God and warned that, if we don't, we will not receive salvation. This is not because obeying the law is earning our salvation, but because it is the route those filled with the Spirit will walk on their way to heaven, just as Noah's route was to build an ark. Or, we might say that one of the signs of a true disciple is that they will love the law. David sang that the law was sweeter than honey, more precious than gold, and that keeping it would bring reward (Psalm 19). Jesus taught that "if you keep my commandments, you will abide in my love" (John 15:10). Neither Jesus nor David are legalists; both know that obedience is the path to salvation. And this law is not a burden, but a gift. It's not so much that we have to obey, as that now, filled with the Spirit of Jesus, we get to obey. Holiness is not a curse, but a reward.

Relating to God through Covenant

So, does God care or not when I disobey the law? Have you ever heard the illustration where a preacher describes two days in the life of a typical Christian? On Monday, Jeff springs out of bed, brings his beautiful wife Caroline breakfast, has an hour of prayer, nips next door to feed Seamus the neighbor's cat, evangelizes his fellow passengers on the bus, works hard all day, gives some of his bonus earnings to a mission organization, and gets home just in time to lead an inspiring Bible study on Isaiah. The next day, he gets up late, ignores his Bible, swears at his neighbor, is rude to his boss, and skips the prayer meeting to stay in and watch a dodgy movie. "On which day is God more pleased with Jeff?" asks the preacher. "They're both the same!" he answers. "God's love is unconditional! He sees us in Christ! We are justified! Our works no longer matter!" Is he right?

Well, yes and no. This is where recovering a more covenantal way of thinking, with its emphasis on union with Christ, will help us stay balanced. On the one hand, when I remember that I now share Jesus' status, justified and fully pleasing in God's sight, I can rejoice that, no matter how bad I've been today, God still loves me as his child and will accept me into heaven. My justification is unchangeable, unspoilable—and, for that matter, unimprovable.

But if this is my *only* understanding of how God views me, then I'm likely to get in a muddle when I come across passages in the Bible that suggest God reacts to how I live. There are those passages that talk about God rewarding people who live holy lives, passages that speak of certain actions pleasing him. Conversely, there are passages that speak of God disciplining Christians who disobey, and even some where he causes believers to get ill and die because of their unholy lives.[8] None of these will make any sense if I only ever think of justification; after all, if God sees Jesus and not me, surely it's impossible for his opinion of me to change for better or for worse?

But when I remember that God also sees my sanctification, suddenly things make sense. God will assess how serious I have been about trying to be faithful to his covenant: repenting, believing, battling sin, walking in holiness. If I start to ignore him, then he has every right to come and discipline. Equally, if I'm faithful, I can genuinely please him and he will reward me—most likely in eternity, but possibly in the short term as well.[9] These rewards differ between believers, a sure sign that God will take account of how faithfully we have walked.[10] Sure, every Christian ends up in heaven, but our experiences of heaven will differ. We'll all be happy and satisfied, yet some even more so than others. It's a bit like filling an eggcup, a wine glass, and a bucket with water. They're all full, but the bucket is also in a sense fuller than the others!

To put it another way, it is possible to be a covenant-keeper in the primary sense, a person of faith who is going to heaven, while at a secondary level be wandering off-course into paths of covenant disobedience. As we saw earlier with the Israelites and Solomon, God often intervenes in his people's lives to discipline them long before judgment day. If he sees us wandering from covenant faithfulness, he might give us a little taste of what complete disobedience would bring, in order to bring us back to our senses. Many of the seven churches in the book of Revelation experience just such warnings. If I or my church begin to suffer these kinds of warning signs, we need to wake up and return to God.

If this does happen, I'll need to remember I'm not back under the covenant of works again, and that Christ alone is my righteousness. I'll therefore respond first and foremost by repenting and believing the gospel promises again, rather than simply trying to sort myself out. Only after I've gone to God for forgiveness, can I, through his strength and encouraged by his love, begin to make progress in my holiness battles.

Being under the covenant of grace, not works, means that every single action God takes toward me, without exception, will ultimately be an act of love. Yes, even discipline: God disciplines those whom he loves.[11]

If I forget the legal, justification side of union with Christ, I'll find myself falling into a kind of sub-Christian karma—be good and God will bless you; be bad and he'll get you. If I forget the organic, sanctification side of union with Christ, I'll end up thinking how I live is completely irrelevant, and fail to listen to the many different passages in the Bible that tell me otherwise. Legal bond and organic bond, justification and sanctification: all inseparable fruits of union with Christ.

The End Is Just the Beginning

And so, as we come to the end, we can see why the end is better than the beginning. God's new world will be full of people who are in turn full of the Spirit of Jesus. At the start of the story, Adam was not connected to Jesus as the vine. He was not glorified, so he was still able to sin and die. When Jesus completes his transformation of his people, they will be in a far better state than simply being sinless—they will be so full of the Spirit they will no longer even dream of disobeying God.

This is your future if you're a Christian. You cannot spoil heaven: God is more powerful than your sin, and he will one day destroy it for ever. That day won't come until you die or Jesus returns, but, when he does come back and bring in the final chapter of covenant history, we will be at the beginning of another story far greater than anything we've yet imagined. And the wonderful news is that even then things won't be "perfect" in the sense of static, finished, and complete. God is so immense that there will always be greater wonders to explore, always new riches to experience. The end is just the beginning. No wonder the Bible closes with a simple prayer: "Come, Lord Jesus! . . . Amen" (Revelation 22:20–21).

NOTES

Chapter 1: The Covenant of Works

1 These quotes are all from Packer's introduction to Herman Witsius, *The Economy of the Covenants between God and Man*, available online at http://gospelpedlar.com/articles/Bible/cov_theo.html.

2 The people, place, presence framework is far from original. Most recently it has been promoted by Graeme Goldsworthy in books such as *Gospel and Kingdom* (Paternoster Press, 1994) and *According to Plan* (IVP, 2003), and simplified in Vaughan Roberts' *God's Big Picture* (IVP, 2009). The focus in these works tends to be more on kingdom than covenant.

3 H. Bavinck, *Reformed Dogmatics*, ed. John Bolt, trans. John Vriend, 4 vols. (Grand Rapids, MI: Baker Academic, 2003–2008), vol. 2, p. 564.

4 Similarly, many Bible overviews have traced the theme of kingdom through the Bible, and found its roots in Eden. This is entirely valid, but, like "covenant," the term "kingdom" is missing from Genesis 1–3 and indeed is not explicitly used of God's people until the book of Exodus. I'm grateful to David Gibson for this point.

5 This mirrors the pattern later with Abraham. When God begins his covenant relationship with Abraham, the covenant is "cut" (Genesis 15:18), but when he returns a couple of chapters later to restate and develop the covenant, the word is "established," just as in Genesis 6. Cf. too Jeremiah 33:20–25.

Chapter 2: Covenant Cursed

1 Available online at http://www.ccel.org/ccel/calvin/calcom01 .ix.i.html (accessed 22 May 2013).

2 Henri Blocher, *In the Beginning: The Opening Chapters of Genesis* (IVP, 1984), p. 176.

3 G. K. Chesterton, *Orthodoxy* (1908), ch. 2. Available online at www.gutenberg.org.

Chapter 3: Covenant Conflict

1 Herman Bavinck even talks about Adam and Eve being in covenant with Satan.

Chapter 5: Moses and Covenant Obedience

1 Incidentally, when this exile does arrive, Israel heads east out of Israel to Babylon, just as Adam and Eve were sent east out of Eden. Fascinatingly, when the Israelites first enter the Promised Land, they come not from the south as would be logical from Egypt, but circle to come from east to west. Similarly, the tabernacle was always to be set up so that, as an Israelite came through the door, he or she was moving from east to west: symbolically back to Eden and God's presence. Likewise, in the calling of Abraham, God sends his people from the east to the west: it seems that even the Bible's geography has something to teach us!

2 Historically, this position has often been associated with Lutheran writers. Modern Reformed writers like Meredith Kline and Michael Horton also argue that this covenant, while not intended to grant

eternal life, was nevertheless a kind of "republication" of the covenant of works. This time, though, it was merely a temporary arrangement dealing with the nation of Israel. If Israel obeyed, they would be blessed; if they disobeyed, they would be cursed. It was a strict "merit-your-own-reward" set-up, very different from the covenant with Abraham, where the condition was faith.

3 See M. Horton, *God of Promise* (P&R, 2006) or the collection of essays in Bryan Estelle, J. V. Fesko, David VanDrunen (eds.), *The Law Is Not of Faith* (P&R, 2009) for introductions to this position from some Reformed thinkers. Somewhat strangely (in my view!), Kline and some in his camp think God would have accepted the reaching of a certain imperfect obedience to the Mosaic covenant as good enough for Israel to earn the physical blessings of the land promised at Sinai.

4 Herman Bavinck, *Reformed Dogmatics*, ed. John Bolt, trans. John Vriend, 4 vols. (Grand Rapids, MI: Baker Academic, 2003–2008), vol. 3, p. 220.

Chapter 6: David and the Covenant King

1 I pinched this phrase from a sermon extract by Douglas Wilson, available on www.canonwired.com.

Chapter 7: The New Covenant

1 See for example Isaiah 49; 52.

2 Isaiah 11:6–9; 65:17–25; Habakkuk 2:14.

3 I am grateful to Bruce Ware for this illustration from his fascinating addresses on the humanity of Christ at New Word Alive 2013—and for permission to steal it!

4 It's worth remembering that not every prophecy of the new covenant necessarily uses the specific term: almost all the prophets look forward to the great day of the Lord, which in several places is also explained as the day the new covenant comes into being.

5 This may come as a surprise to some—especially dispensationalists and Yorkshire men.

6 Hence the question of the State of Israel is *primarily* a political rather than religious one for Christians. There is no special biblical mandate for Christians to campaign for, or indeed expect, an earthly restoration of the Old Testament land of Israel. The promises of the one covenant create one people for God, who will all together inherit the whole earth.

7 Though Jesus says the marriage and child-raising aspects of the cultural mandate will no longer continue. See Mark 12:24–26.

8 John Newton, "Amazing Grace" (1779). Again this fact was pointed out to me by a friend from church, Dom Sant.

Chapter 8: The Covenant of Redemption

1 John Henry Newman, "Praise to the Holiest in the Height" (1865).

2 John Calvin, *Institutes of the Christian Religion* 3.1.1 (first published 1536).

3 John Eddison (1916–2011), "At the Cross of Jesus."

Chapter 9: Covenant Salvation

1 Limited atonement doesn't necessarily imply a small number will be saved. Reformed theologians disagree among themselves here, but it is at least possible that God could create 100 billion people, save 95 billion, and leave 5 billion to their rebellion: that way heaven would be far more full than hell. In this case, the atonement would be "limited" to 95% of humanity!

2 This position is often driven by a healthy desire to do justice to texts where Jesus is said to die for "all" or for "the world." While there is no space here to deal with specific verses, we can briefly note that "world" often means not "every single person" but rather "rebels against God." These verses are therefore not about the number of people Jesus saves but the type: "world" is an ethical term. Jesus

dying for "all" verses are usually to do with the idea that Jesus' death is not just for Jews but for Gentiles too.

3 Shai Linne, "Mission Accomplished," from the album *The Atonement*, Lamp Mode Recordings, 2008. Used by permission.

4 This way of framing the question comes from D. Wilson, *Easy Chairs, Hard Words* (Canon Press, 1991). The book is written as a conversation between a Reformed pastor and a young student, a device that enables Wilson to wrestle with many of the questions we want to ask about God's sovereignty.

Chapter 10: Covenant People

1 One of the problems with the Baptist position is that it tries to get rid of the category of New Testament covenant-breaking. While Baptists acknowledge this was possible in the Old Covenant, the New is in their opinion unbreakable. But this leads us into difficulty when we come across passages such as 2 Peter 2:1 discussed above. Compare too Hebrews 6 and 10:26–30.

Chapter 11: Covenant Life

1 Acts 2:41; Exodus 32:25–28.

2 This is a large part of the argument of Romans. See Romans 3 in particular.

3 This seems to be the point of the tricky passage in 2 Corinthians 3.

4 Paul battles this issue in Galatians, especially chapters 3–4.

5 Mark 7:19.

6 Deuteronomy 23:24.

7 The most debated commandment is the Sabbath. Some think that this was a temporary institution for the era of Moses, a sign now fulfilled in the rest from self-justification that Jesus brings. It seems though that Israel kept the Sabbath before they were given the commandments. For example, they were told not to collect manna on the Sabbath, in an episode set four chapters before the giving of

the law at Sinai (see Exodus 16:23–29). This suggests it is a command for all eras of covenant history, though now honored in a different way. With the resurrection of Jesus, the day moved from the seventh to the first day of the week (see Acts 20:7; 1 Corinthians 16:2; Revelation 1:10).

8 See 1 Corinthians 11:17–34.

9 See Mark 10:28–30 for one example.

10 Luke 19:11–19; 2 Corinthians 5:10.

11 Hebrews 12:6.

FURTHER READING FOR
SEEING THE GOSPEL AFRESH

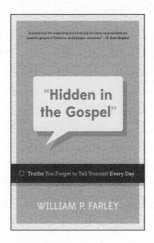

The gospel: a story beginning before time and stretching into eternity, relevant to every stage of your spiritual life. Learn how to apply its truths to every moment each day.

"This small gem of a book provides a joyous gospel feast that begins with our election in Christ before the foundation of the world and ends with Christ's new creation. No small thoughts here! This is the recipe for big, expansive, and ever-expanding hearts."
   —*R. Kent Hughes*

MORE BIBLE GUIDES FROM P&R PUBLISHING

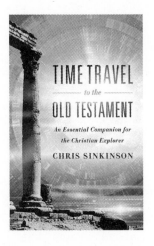

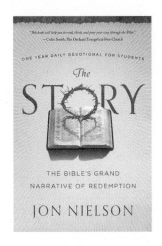

Time Travel to the Old Testament is a wide-ranging, lively introduction to the Old Testament's storytelling techniques, laws, people, beliefs, and geography. This guide puts puzzling details in their historical context—deepening your understanding and appreciation.

The Story is a yearlong, daily study of God's Word that guides you through five acts of his grand story of redemption. Daily Scripture and devotional readings will equip you to understand the unity and development of God's story and to grow in your personal discipline of Bible study and prayer.

MORE FROM P&R PUBLISHING ON LAW, GRACE, AND THE GOSPEL

Why do Christians—even mature Christians—still sin so often? Why doesn't God set us free? Speaking from her own struggles, Barbara Duguid turns to the writings of John Newton to teach us God's purpose for our failure and guilt—and to help us adjust our expectations of ourselves. Rediscover how God's extravagant grace makes the gospel once again feel like the good news it truly is!

"I cannot commend this book enough. We need more and more books like this that remind us that the focus of the Christian faith is not the life of the Christian, but Christ."
    —*Tullian Tchividjian*

CHRIST-CENTERED STUDIES OF THE OLD TESTAMENT FROM P&R PUBLISHING

 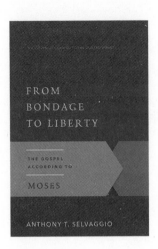

"A tremendous resource." —*Tim Keller*

Written for laypeople and pastors, The Gospel According to the Old Testament series examines the lives of Old Testament characters. It is designed to encourage Christ-centered reading, teaching, and preaching of the Old Testament.

ALSO IN THE SERIES:

After God's Own Heart, Mark J. Boda

Crying Out for Vindication, David R. Jackson

Faith in the Face of Apostasy, Raymond B. Dillard

From Famine to Fullness, Dean R. Ulrich

Hope in the Midst of a Hostile World, George M. Schwab

Immanuel in Our Place, Tremper Longman III

Living in the Gap between Promise and Reality, Iain M. Duguid

Living in the Grip of Relentless Grace, Iain M. Duguid

Living in the Light of Inextinguishable Hope, Iain M. Duguid

Longing for God in an Age of Discouragement, Bryan Gregory

Love Divine and Unfailing, Michael P. V. Barrett

Right in Their Own Eyes, George M. Schwab

Salvation Through Judgment and Mercy, Brian D. Estelle

FOUNDATIONAL RESOURCES
FROM P&R PUBLISHING

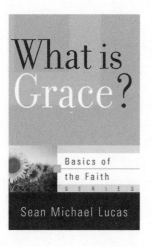

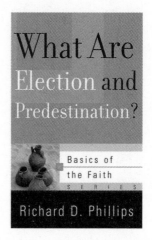

Basics of the Faith booklets introduce readers to basic Reformed doctrine and practice. On issues of church government and practice they reflect that framework—otherwise they are suitable for all church situations.

MORE BOOKLETS IN THE SERIES:

Is Jesus in the Old Testament?

What Are Spiritual Gifts?

What Is Church Government?

What Is Evangelism?

What Is Faith?

What Is Hell?

What Is Justification by Faith Alone?

What Is Man?

What Is Perseverance of the Saints?

What Is Providence?

What Is Spiritual Warfare?

What Is the Atonement?

What Is the Incarnation?

What Is the Lord's Supper?

What Is the Trinity?

What Is True Conversion?

What Is Resurrection?

Why Do We Baptize Infants?